37-71

THE AUTHOR

Ronny Adhikarya is a Fellow at the East-West Communication Institute, Honolulu, working on a Communication Planning and Policy project. Born in Bogor, Indonesia in 1949, he was educated in Indonesia, graduated in sociology and social science from the State University of New York and in 1972 received a Master of Communication Arts from Cornell University Graduate School. He is an experienced journalist, photographer and editor, has travelled widely and has received numerous research awards. He has been Assistant Professor of Communication at University Science Malaysia, and from 1972 to 1974 was staff researcher at the East-West Communication Institute. He has also served as communication consultant to various international agencies working in Asia, the Middle East and North Africa, in the area of rural development.

ISBN 0 7100 8530 3. Printed in Great Britain. (TY). For copyright reasons, this book may not be sold or issued on loan or otherwise disposed of except in its original paper cover.

BROADCASTING IN
PENINSULAR MALAYSIA

Other volumes in this series include

'Broadcasting in Sweden': Edward W. Ploman
                           with Sveriges Radio

'Broadcasting in Canada': E.S. Hallman
                           with H. Hindley

BROADCASTING IN PENINSULAR MALAYSIA

Ronny Adhikarya
with Woon Ai Leng
      Wong Hock Seng
      Khor Yoke Lim

CASE STUDIES ON BROADCASTING SYSTEMS

ROUTLEDGE & KEGAN PAUL
London, Henley and Boston
in association with
INTERNATIONAL INSTITUTE OF COMMUNICATIONS

First published in 1977
by Routledge & Kegan Paul Ltd
39 Store Street,
London WC1E 7DD,
Reading Road,
Henley-on-Thames,
Oxon RG9 1EN and
9 Park Street,
Boston, Mass. 02108, USA
Manuscript typed by Vera M. Taggart
Printed and bound in Great Britain
by Unwin Brothers Limited,
The Gresham Press, Old Woking, Surrey
A member of the Staples Printing Group

ISBN   0 7100 8530 3

CONTENTS

FOREWORD by Asa Briggs   vii

ACKNOWLEDGMENTS   xi

1 NATIONAL ENVIRONMENT FOR BROADCASTING   1
   1 Malaysia's social, economic and political
      structures   1
   2 Malaysia's mass media structure   5
   3 Telecommunications activities   14
   4 National education system   21

2 DEVELOPMENT OF BROADCASTING:
   HISTORICAL PERSPECTIVE   27
   1 Radio   27
   2 Television   30

3 REGULATIONS AND POLICIES FOR
   BROADCASTING OPERATIONS   33
   1 General objectives and goals   33
   2 Legal relationships   33
   3 Policies on advisory board   34
   4 Transmission policies   34
   5 Coverage policies   35
   6 Policies on content of programmes   36
   7 Policies on educational broadcasting   39
   8 Official/formal control mechanisms   39
   9 Financing policies   40
  10 Co-ordination policies   41
  11 Operational relationships between
      broadcasting agencies and other bodies   41
  12 Managerial recruitment policies   42
  13 Policies on employment procedures   43
  14 Policies on international loans/aids   43
  15 Regulations and foreign imports   44

16 Policies on training   45
17 Policies on research   46

4 ORGANISATION AND PROCESSES OF THE DEPARTMENT
   OF BROADCASTING (RTM)   47
   1 Objectives and goals   47
   2 Coverage   48
   3 Laws and regulations   53
   4 Relationships with other
      national organisations   53
   5 Public relations and co-ordinating
      activities   55
   6 Finance   57
   7 Broadcasting output   58
   8 Production   61
   9 Organisation of technical services   61
  10 Administration   65
  11 Training by the organisation   69
  12 Training by other bodies   73
  13 Research   77

5 ORGANISATION AND PROCESSES OF THE RADIO
   ROYAL AUSTRALIAN AIR FORCE, Butterworth   78

6 ORGANISATION AND PROCESSES OF THE
   EDUCATIONAL MEDIA SERVICE   81
   1 General objectives and functions   81
   2 Coverage   82
   3 Laws and regulations   82
   4 Relationships with other national
      organisations/public relations activities   82
   5 Finance   83
   6 Broadcast output   84
   7 Administration   85
   8 Training   88
   9 Research   89

7 ORGANISATION AND PROCESSES OF REDIFFUSION   90

8 EVOLUTION IN THE FUTURE   94
   1 New programmes   94
   2 Going colour   95
   3 National transmission via satellite   95

9 COMMUNICATION POLICIES   97

   APPENDIX - Maps   99

   BIBLIOGRAPHY   101

FOREWORD

In many different parts of the world official and
unofficial enquiries, often protracted, are being carried
out concerning the future of broadcasting. In every case
two points almost immediately become clear. First, the
future of broadcasting can never be completely separated
from its past, even though that past in all countries is
a recent one: there may be sharp breaks but there are
also continuities. Second, the future, like the past,
will not depend on technological development alone.
There are many exciting new communications technologies,
many of them still in their early stages, but the speed
and scope of their development will be determined by
social, economic, political and cultural factors as well
as by the technologies themselves. It has always been so.

Common technologies have been employed in different
ways in different countries - sometimes with few control
systems imposed by governments or by professional groups,
often with many. It is remarkable to what a great extent
it is necessary to understand the general history of countries in order to understand what they have done with
their conscious or unconscious communications policies.

This series of monographs, sponsored by the International Institute of Communications is intended to direct
attention to the main features of the communications patterns of a number of different countries. The studies
deal with broadcasting structures rather than with the
detailed processes of programme making or with the diffusion of news and ideas; and they seek first to explain
how these structures came into existence, second, to
identify what have been the landmarks in their histories
and, third, to elucidate what are the alternative possi-
bilities envisaged for the future. Of course, a knowledge

of the structures by itself is not enough to enable an
adequate evaluation to be made of the quality of broadcasting output in any particular case. The same structure
will generate different output at different times, and
very similar structures will generate very different outputs.

Until recently it was thought possible to distinguish
broadly between on the one hand systems controlled by
government and on the other hand systems linked to business through private enterprise and advertising. Yet
there was always a third type of system, represented
formidably by the BBC, where there was neither government
control nor business underpinning it. This system, which
was widely copied, was seldom copied in its entirety, and
it now has many variants. In many countries also there
are now dual or multiple systems, in some cases, but not
all, subject to common 'supervision'; and in all countries
there are degrees and nuances of control whether by governments or by market forces.

The United States system, which is important not only
in itself but because of the influence it has through
exports of programmes and through diffusion of broadcasting
styles, is itself a complex system - containing as it does
a multiplicity of agencies and a changing public service
element. It is hoped that United States experience will
be covered in a later volume.

Alongside such complex structures, the products of time
and place and in many cases deeply resistant to fundamen-
tal change, there are, of course, many new broadcasting
structures in the world, including many which have come
into existence in new countries.

Many of these structures reveal themselves as extremely
complex, too, when they are subjected to careful scrutiny.
Nor are they necessarily very malleable. The more governments set out to chart and carry through conscious 'communications policies' - often related directly to their
planning policies - the more they are compelled to con-
sider the relationship of 'traditional' modes of communication to new technologies. The more, too, they are
forced to establish priorities. This series will include,
therefore, a number of cases where such policies have been
formulated or are in the course of formulation.

Measuring the distance between policy formulation and
policy implementation or effectiveness is, of course, at

least as difficult in this field as in any other, and
interesting work is being carried out by scholars in
several countries on promise and performance. These
studies are not so ambitious. They are designed to provide easily accessible information about a wide variety
of cases (including cases where market forces are the main
influence on what happens) and to cover big and small and
old and new countries alike. The first cases chosen
include some where there is no existing manageable mono-
graph and some where the experience of that country is of
particular general interest at the present time. As the
series unfolds, there will be increasing scope for comparison and contrast, and international patterns will
doubtless be revealed - of 'models', 'imports' and
'exports', and of regional 'exchanges'. If it is likely
that such comparison and contrast will become more sophis-
ticated than it has been in the past, it is at the same
time certain that it will be of increasing value in the
future of those policy-makers who are concerned to frame
their choices clearly and to see their own circumstances
in perspective.

Meanwhile, the International Institute of Communications,which has sponsored this series, will continue to
concern itself also with the general opportunities and
problems associated with the continuing advance of communications technology. The Institute is an international body which seeks to bring together engineers and
social scientists, lawyers and programme-makers, aca-
demics and administrators.

The author of each case study in this series has been
free to assemble and present material relating to his own
country in a manner decided upon by him, and he alone is
responsible for the evidence presented and the conclusions
drawn. Yet guidelines have been given him about arrange-
ment and coverage. Thus, he has been encouraged to ask
such questions as what have been the critical points in
the history of broadcasting; how has that history and the
broadcasting structures which have evolved been related
to the history of other forms of communication (the press,
for example); what are the main institutional relationships at the present time; what are likely to be the future trends; and whether it is possible to talk of an
integrated 'communications policy' in that particular
case.

The International Institute of Communications as an
institution has no views of its own on the answers to such

questions, but its trustees and members believe that
answers should be forthcoming. Much of the serious study
of communications systems has been carried out within the
confines, cultural as well as political, of national boun-
daries, and it is such research which most easily secures
financial support. This series will point in a different
direction. It is not only comparison and contrast which
are necessary but a grasp of what problems and opportunities are common to countries, not necessarily alone but
in the great continental broadcasting unions or other
groupings.

We can now trace the beginning of a 'global' sense in
communications studies. Indeed, the word 'beginning' may
be misleading. The sense certainly long preceded the use
of satellites and was anticipated in much of the nine-
teenth-century literature. The world was being pulled
together: it was becoming a smaller place: everyone
everywhere would be drawn in.

Communications policies have often, of course, pulled
people apart in clashes of images as well as wars of
words. And some of the case studies in this series will
show how.

Two final points should be made. First, nothing stands
still in communications history and there are bound to be
changes between the writing of these case studies and
their publication. Second, because the British case is at
present under review, treatment of it in this series is
being deferred. Meanwhile, the first three studies come
from three different continents and some of the structures
are the newest of all.

Asa Briggs
Chairman, IIC Research Panel

ACKNOWLEDGMENTS

The International Institute of Communications and the
authors gratefully acknowledge the co-operation of the
organisations and many individuals in Malaysia who
assisted in the preparation of this case study. Special
mention, however, should be made of Mr Harun Din, Deputy
Secretary-General, Ministry of Information, Mr Abdullah
bin Mohamad, Director-General of Broadcasting, and
Mr R. Balakrishnan, Director, National Broadcasting
Training Centre, who have not only given their assistance
but also enthusiasm and encouragement.

Chapter 1

NATIONAL ENVIRONMENT FOR BROADCASTING

1 MALAYSIA'S SOCIAL, ECONOMIC AND POLITICAL STRUCTURES

Malaysia is a federation of 13 states. It was established
on 16 September 1963 and comprises the 11 states in
Peninsular Malaysia (West Malaysia) and Sarawak and Sabah
(East Malaysia) in Borneo. The total land area of
Malaysia is 127,670 square miles. The area of Peninsular
Malaysia is about 52,000 square miles.

According to 1974 estimates, the population of Malaysia
was 11.62 million - 9.77 million in Peninsular Malaysia
and 1.83 million in East Malaysia.

The Federal Parliament is the supreme legislative
authority in Malaysia. A general election is held every
5 years. The Head of State is the Yang di-Pertuan Agung
(King or Supreme Sovereign) who is elected by the other
rulers of the states at a Conference of Rulers, to serve
for 5 years.

The Head of State together with the two Dewans (Houses
of Parliament) namely, the Dewan Negara (Senate) and the
Dewan Rakyat (House of Representatives) make up the
Federal Parliament.

The economy

Peninsular Malaysia's economic wealth is primarily derived
from rubber and tin, and East Malaysia's from timber. The
modern sector of Malaysia is situated in the west-coast
region of Peninsular Malaysia where there has been rapid
progress in industrialisation, construction and services.
Peninsular Malaysia is rapidly switching from a traditional agriculture-based economy to an agro-industrial one.

The Gross National Product (GNP) per capita in Malaysia
is about M$1,680 (US$700), one of the highest in Asia.
The annual GNP growth rate at constant prices for 1974 was
6 per cent, which is relatively high, though it is below
the previous years' growth rates. This is largely due to
the recession in industrial countries and the subsequent
decline in demand for Malaysia's primary commodities.

The government has tried to strengthen the economy by
both agricultural and industrial diversification. Oil
palm, cocoa, pepper, sugarcane are some of the crops
introduced under the agricultural diversification programme. But rubber is still the country's mainstay,
accounting for more than 17 per cent of the country's
Gross Domestic Product (GDP). Agriculture provided 54 per
cent of the country's export earnings in 1974, of which
more than half was provided by rubber alone.

The manufacturing sector has expanded rapidly with
government incentives. It now contributes 16 per cent to
the country's GDP, and is expected to make even more sub-
stantial contributions in the future.

Total employment in 1974 was about 3.8 million. The
main source of employment is still the agricultural sector with 48 per cent of total employment. Unemployment
causes serious concern. The unemployment rate declined
from 7.5 per cent in 1970 to 7.3 per cent in 1973 but
then rose again because of the world-wide recession. New
jobs are expected, however, in the manufacturing sector
which accounted for about 11 per cent of total employment
in 1974.

A plural society

Malaysia is a multi-racial society. Of the total 1972
population of 9,319,927 in Peninsular Malaysia, the
Malays numbered 4,991,405 (53.56 per cent), Chinese
3,325,595 (35.68 per cent), Indians 929,679 (9.97 per
cent) and other races about 73,248 (0.79 per cent).

This plurality is due largely to the British colonial
policy of importing, or at least encouraging, Chinese and
Indian labourers to work the tin mines and rubber estates,
and leaving the Malays' basically agricultural life undis-
turbed. While the development of the tin and rubber sectors was encouraged, together with the infrastructure of
importers, exporters, traders, middlemen, etc. the rest of
the economic base was neglected.

The outcome of this policy was that the Chinese in particular began to have greater control over the economy.
Their accumulated capital and business acumen enabled them
to expand with the economy. The Malays on the other hand
were still tied to the land. The indirect rule practised
by the British also accounted for economic and political
power not being in the hands of any one race. Until very
recently the usual assumption was that economic power lay
with the Chinese while political power lay with the
Malays.

It is probable, therefore, that the separation of the
races within the economic and political systems of Malaysia was the result of British colonial policy. This separation could be one of the reasons why the major races of
Malaysia remain individual communities rather than one
people, with different aims about their own and their
country's future. These differences were perhaps the main
factors that led to the racial riots in the capital city,
Kuala Lumpur, in May 1969; the consequences of which led
to new economic and political policies aimed at uniting
the people.

Political development

The main problems facing the Malaysian government therefore are: the development of the agricultural and industrial sectors of the economy; the creation of a united
society with a common goal; and the correction of racial
imbalances in the economy which are the legacies of colonial rule.

Following the 1969 riots, Parliament was temporarily
suspended and a National Operations Council (NOC) formed.
The Council relied on the political support of the Malays
but also depended upon the enterprise of the Chinese and
Indians to maintain and accelerate Malaysia's economic
growth. It was losing Malay political support, however,
because of the Malays' growing socio-economic frustrations
and fears of a Chinese challenge to their political hege-
mony. The non-Malays, on the other hand, resented the
perpetuation of the position and status of the Sultans and
the King, the establishment of Islam as the state religion, the adoption of Malay as the national language and
the fear that their own cultures would be threatened by
Malaysianisation (see M. Rogers, 'Malaysia/Singapore:
Problems and challenges of the seventies', p.122).

The National Consultative Council (NCC) was formed in
1970 to examine political, economic and cultural problems
affecting national unity and to formulate guidelines for
promoting social integration and the growth of a Malaysian
sense of national identity. The government felt that
agreement on two basic issues must be reached before
parliamentary democracy could be restored:
a)   a proposed national ideology and
b)   the disparity of incomes between ethnic groups and its
     effects upon national unity (see M. Rogers, op. cit.,
     p. 122).

The Malay-led NOC also felt that a return to parliamentary rule would be disastrous unless the political process
was changed to ensure that certain principles and policies
in the Constitution could not be questioned (ibid.).

In March 1971, the government amended the 1948 Sedition
Act, making it an offence to raise 'sensitive issues'
which might incite communal resentment. The ban prohibits
utterances or printed statements which appear to question:
a)   the special position of the Malays and other indigen-
     ous groups,
b)   Malay as the national language,
c)   the citizenship rights of any ethnic group,
d)   the rights and sovereignty of the Malay rulers.

New political and economic policies

To promote national unity, the government adopted the
national ideology of Rukunegara, which sets forth five
principles: belief in God, loyalty to King and country,
upholding the Constitution, rule of law and good behaviour
and morality. It was hoped that by disallowing statements
or actions offensive to other ethnic groups, the Rukunegara would achieve national unity.

One of the outcomes of the 1969 riots was the New Economic Policy incorporated in the Second Malaysia Plan
1971-75. The policy aimed at national unity with emphasis
on social integration and a more equitable distribution of
income and opportunities. It embodies development plans
designed, according to the government, to eliminate
poverty, to restructure Malaysian society and to correct
racial and economic imbalance.

Under the plan, social and economic development was,
for the first time, seen as a vehicle for national unity

and not as something separate from the life of the nation.
This involved the modernisation of rural life and the bal-
anced growth of urban opportunities for the low-income
groups so that they will be able to participate more fully
in the economic life of the nation. The plan also calls
for 30 per cent Malay participation in all levels of commercial and business activities. This would, of course,
necessitate changing the traditional values of the Malays
to take up the challenge of modernisation and development.

Talking about achieving Malaysia's development plan,
the former Prime Minister, Tun Haji Abdul Razak bin
Hussein, said:

The Government, the private sector, and people from all
walks of life must co-operate fully to implement the
Plan and make it a success. A necessary first step is
understanding and appreciation of the objectives and
strategy of the Plan by all. For its part, the Government will always keep the public and the people
informed of its policies and action, and do everything
possible to assist them. It will also be alert and
responsive to constructive suggestions from any
quarter, which will help in the implementation of the
Plan (Government of Malaysia, 'Highlight of Second
Malaysia Plan', p. 9).

This underlines the important role of the mass media in
Malaysia.

2   MALAYSIA'S MASS MEDIA STRUCTURE

Government mass media:

All government mass media activities are co-ordinated by
the Ministry of Information. The Ministry has two main
divisions: the Department of Broadcasting and the Department of Information.

There are five Ministry guidelines for government communicators and broadcasters:
to explain in depth and with the widest possible coverage
government policies and programmes to ensure maximum
public understanding;
to stimulate public interest and opinion to achieve its
desired changes;
to assist in promoting civic consciousness and fostering
the development of Malaysian arts and culture;
to provide suitable elements of popular education, general
information and entertainment;

to promote national unity - by using Bahasa Malaysia, the national language - in a multi-racial society towards the propagation of a Malaysian culture and identity.

Department of Broadcasting   Also known as RTM (Radio Television Malaysia), this department has its headquarters in the Angkasapuri Complex, Kuala Lumpur.

Angkasapuri accommodates Radio House, TV House and the Administration Building. It cost M$34 million to house the scattered broadcasting units at Angkasapuri in 1968. And the M$13.9 million Wisma Radio added in 1973 made the site the largest broadcasting complex in South East Asia.

The main purpose of Angakasapuri is to present government programmes and policies to the people. The presentation of news in particular is governed by the need to promote national unity in a multi-racial and multi-lingual context. The present policy of developing a Malaysian identity resulted in all announcements being made in Bahasa Malaysia on all channels.

Radio Malaysia operates five networks domestically - National (Bahasa Malaysia), Blue (English), Green (Chinese) and Red (Tamil) Networks and Capital City Broadcasts. It also broadcasts special programmes for the Orang Asli (Aborigines) in the Semai and Temiar dialects. Suara Malaysia (The Voice of Malaysia) broadcasts to overseas listeners in Indonesian, English, Arabic, Mandarin, Thai and Tagalog.

TV Malaysia broadcasts two channels through a network of transmitters within the country's microwave network. Broadcasts are black and white on 625 lines.

The Broadcasting Department has several divisions, headed by a Director-General, and assisted by a secretariat consisting of the Deputy Director-General, Director of Programmes, Director of Engineering, Director of News, Director of Public Affairs, Head of Administration and Head of Finance.

RTM's News Division now has a 24-hour news service. World news comes through wire services and international newsfilm through an agency, Visnews Ltd. Local news is provided by RTM's own reporters and cameramen, plus Bernama (the national news agency). There is also a radiophoto service.

The Engineering Division's operation and maintenance section is responsible for all the engineering facilities while the Design and Development section draws up long-term plans for radio and TV coverage and looks after the implementation of projects.

Within RTM's Programme Division, there are several services shared by both radio and television.

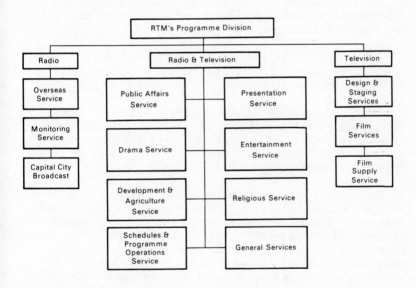

FIGURE 1   Services of RTM's Programme Division

The Public Affairs Service's main task is to 'stimulate public opinion' to achieve changes in line with the aims of government policies. Talks, documentaries, forums, features and interviews are used in campaigns and publicity drives for government departments and statutory bodies. This service also looks after all sports and quiz programmes, and programmes for women and children.

The Presentation Service is responsible for all aspects of presentation over radio and television. Staff news readers and announcers are supplemented by part-timers.

The Entertainment Service's main tasks are to produce 'live' musical programmes for radio and television and to

'discover, encourage and develop' new talent in the field
of music and singing. This includes annual competitions.

The Drama Service is responsible for all locally produced radio and television drama and for all short
stories broadcast over Radio Malaysia.

The Development and Agriculture Service's most important role is to orientate the public to the Government's
New Economic Policy and its Community Development drive.
This Service works closely with government ministries,
departments and semi-government bodies involved with local
and national development projects.

The Religious Service's main function is to promote the
teaching of Islam, the official religion of the country by
producing regular programmes for all levels of society.

The Schedule and Programme Operations Service looks
after programmes' requirements, traffic, operations, programmes' planning and scheduling. A programme requirements section supplies all recording materials like tapes,
cassettes, cartridges and blank discs.

The General Services consist of two sections: Publicity and Public Relations, and Record, Transcription and
Archives. The first handles press publicity, prepares
slogans and announcements, and is responsible for all the
Department's publications. It also liaises with overseas
broadcasting organisations. Of the second, the Record
Library provides programme staff with recorded materials -
transcription discs, commercial discs, transcription tapes
and archive materials.

RTM's Film Division produces films mainly for the
government. Films for home consumption concentrate on
the Second Malaysia Plan; those for foreign use are primarily to publicise and promote Malaysia's image.

The Commercial Division, set up in 1962, deals with
the advertisers, who can sponsor programmes and buy spot
announcements over both media.

By 1975, advertising from radio and television brought
in more than M$16 million (US$7-04 million). Radio and
television licences raised another M$17.01 million (the
annual licence fee for a television set is M$24 and M$12
for radio).

TABLE 1.1   RTM Advertising Revenue

	Radio		Television
Year	M$ (approx)	Year	M$ (approx)
1970	4.1 million	1970	7.6 million
1973	6.3 million	1973	9.8 million

Department of Information   The Department's main function is to establish a two-way exchange between government
and people. It disseminates government information and
gathers feedback reports of public reaction both at
national and state levels.

The Department has offices in all 13 states, each
headed by a Director based in the state capital. The
State Directors use District Information Officers to carry
out campaigns and programmes at ground level.

The Department is headed by a Director-General, assisted by the Deputy Director-General and divisional heads.
The divisions are:

Field Civics and Community Services is the largest
Division whose main function is to explain all aspects of
the country's policies to the public through mobile units.
These units tour the rural areas to disseminate information through civic activities, group discussions, organised talks and cinema shows, explaining the Constitu-
tional Amendments, the Rukunegara, the New Economic Policy
and other current topics. The Division's Drama Troupe,
too, seeks to explain important matters to the public but
in a simpler manner.

The Visual Production Division has four sections:
Publications, Graphics, Exhibitions and the Photo Library
to provide direct service and technical advice to ministries, government departments and quasi-government bodies.

The Publications Division produces regular and ad hoc
publications. The official Year Book, Tou Shih (in
Chinese), Udhayam (in Tamil), Sinar Zaman (in Bahasa
Malaysia) and Gema RTM are some of the regular publications. Ad hoc publication of books, pamphlets, etc. are
used to explain various aspects of Malaysia's social,
economic and political progress and deal with topics like
the Quran Reading Competition, metrication etc.

The Press and Liaison Division issues government statements to the 50 newspapers in Malaysia, Bernama (the
national news agency), the ten foreign news agencies,
representatives of the foreign press and diplomatic missions in Kuala Lumpur.

This division also provides press facilities and materials for national and international events throughout the
country. It also distributes press statements and publications from government offices, statutory bodies and
voluntary organisations.

To ensure that all ministers' activities are covered
by the media, press liaison officers are posted to individual ministries.

2   Private mass media

Newspapers   Malaysia is well provided for in terms of
newspapers.   Dailies and Sundays total 50, with 12
English, 25 Chinese, 6 Malay, 5 Tamil and 2 Punjabi
papers, selling a total of more than a million copies
each day in East and Peninsular Malaysia.   Peninsular
Malaysia alone has 31 newspapers.

The Chinese language press commands the highest circulation - 800,000 in 1973 (with weekly and Sunday
editions counted as separate papers), compared to
500,000 for the English press, 300,000 for the Malay,
and 100,000 for the Tamil.   However, circulation figures
in themselves are not a true indication of readership.
Readership of the Malay press is particularly high (both
Rumi and Jawi) because of the group reading habits,
indicated in table 1.2.

TABLE 1.2   Level of saturation of Malay newspapers among
adult population

Newspapers	Readers per copy among adult population
Berita Harian	13
Berita Minggu	9
Utusan Melayu	9

Source: Survey Research Malaysia (SRM) Media Index: 1973
The figures are general estimates.   Very few independent
circulation audits are taken by newspapers at present.

The press in Malaysia, although a private concern, adheres to government policies and hence its news pattern is largely government-orientated.

Cinemas   There are about 50 cinemas in the main market centres (Kuala Lumpur, Penang and Ipoh) and a further 400 throughout the country. A fifth of Malaysia's population goes to the movies every week. Three-quarters of regular cinema-goers are Chinese, between the ages of 15 and 30.

Magazines and Books   Local publishing is still in its infancy. In the main market centres modern book stores are gradually increasing in number, stocked mainly with the paperbacks familiar throughout the world. Books on current affairs are among the most popular here; and despite the national language policy, there is a steady growth in the English language market. 'Book Distributors', one of the biggest importers, now has a turnover of between 30,000 and 40,000 paperbacks a month.

A major area of business for the 60-plus local book publishers is in school textbooks, which accounted for M$62 million by the end of 1974. More than 30 per cent of this government-financed market is taken by the government agency Dewan Bahasa dan Pustaka (Language and Literary Agency). About 70 per cent of the industry depends on this market. The Dewan, established as a government department in 1956 and converted to a corporation in 1959, prints books, magazines, pamphlets and other forms of literature, mainly in Bahasa Malaysia.

Dewan Bahasa dan Pustaka takes a big slice of the educational and literary magazine fields in the national language, but the English language publications still hold the monopoly on advertising.

The total of local and imported magazines in the country is estimated to be approaching 200. The pace-setters tend to be the newspaper publishing houses, especially the New Straits Times Press, the Utusan Melayu Group and Star Publications. The magazines published by the government are for the purpose of explaining government policy to the people, aiding national unity or publicising radio and television programmes. The publications division of the Ministry of Information produce more than thirty magazines with a total circulation nearing 3 million. These are mainly in Bahasa Malaysia, with translated versions in English, Mandarin and Tamil.

'Malaysian Panorama' and 'Malaysia in Brief', are
glossy, well-illustrated magazines, produced by the
Ministry of Foreign Affairs for tourists and foreign
businessmen.

A large number of magazines in English are imported
from Hong Kong and elsewhere, among them 'The Asia Magazine', the Asia edition of the 'Reader's Digest', the 'Far
Eastern Economic Review', 'Time', 'Newsweek', etc.

3   Regulatory frames on Malaysian mass media

The laws regulating the mass media are equally applicable
to print and broadcast media. In reality, however, they
are intended to control the press as broadcasting is
undertaken directly by the government. Until 1971, when
the Sedition Act was amended, laws concerning freedom of
the press were rather vague although potentially very
strict as the more important ones had been enacted to
deal with situations arising from the 1948-60 Communist
Emergency. The most important laws are:

The Printing Presses Act (1948)   This Act ensures
that no press can be kept or used without a licence and
that no newspaper can be published or printed without a
government permit, the granting of which may have conditions attached. Licences and permits are granted, and
may be withdrawn, at the discretion of the Home Affairs
Minister and must be renewed yearly.

Since 1970, after the May 1969 riots, the Act also
requires that incidents relating to public order in any
part of Malaysia should not be distorted and that the presentation of these incidents should not incur communal
hostility. No newspaper shall publish articles or photo-
graphs prejudicial to public interest or national security.
The Printing Presses Act was amended in January 1974
to ensure that Malaysian investments in newspapers
exceeded those of non-Malaysians and gave the Home Affairs
Minister power to refuse, suspend or revoke the annual
licence where necessary. This amendment was the result of
increasing government concern in the early 1970s about
ownership patterns in newspapers, which the government
felt did not always help reflect current national aspira-
tions. The 'Straits Times', for instance, one of the
country's oldest papers and certainly the best known and
biggest, reconstituted itself in September 1972 as a
result of official pressure. A new company, the New

Straits Times Press (Malaysia) was formed with 80 per cent
of its shares reserved for Malaysians. The publishing
operations of the group, which hitherto had effectively
produced two editions of the same paper in Kuala Lumpur
and Singapore were completely separated between the two
countries. Other papers, notably the 'Nanyang Siang Pau'
and the 'Sin Chew Jit Poh', the leading Chinese-language
papers, are currently considering similar ownership
changes.

The Internal Security Act (1960)   This Act states that
the Minister in charge (Home Affairs usually), may
    prohibit the printing, publication, sale, issue,
    circulation or possession of any document or publica-
    tion which to him stimulates violence, disobedience to
    laws, or which is likely to lead to a breach of the
    peace or to be prejudicial to the national interest.

Section 28 of the Act reads that
    any person who by word of mouth or in writing or in
    any newspaper, periodical, book or circular or other
    printed publication or by any other means spreads
    false reports or makes false statements likely to
    cause public alarm shall be guilty of an offence.
This applies regardless of the accused's knowledge of
the crime. Section 22(1) of the Act provides that a
Minister may prohibit any publication prejudicial to the
national interest.

The Sedition Act (1948)   This Act states that a person
is liable to imprisonment and fine for any act, speech,
word, publication or other things which tend to:
a) bring into hatred or contempt or to excite disaffect-
    ion against any ruler or against any Government;
b) excite inhabitants of any territory to change any
    laws other than by lawful means;
c) bring into hatred or contempt or to excite disaffect-
    ion against the administration of justice in the
    Federation or in any other state;
d) raise discontent or disaffection against subjects of
    His Majesty or any other ruler of any state and its
    inhabitants;
e) promote feelings of ill-will and hostility between
    different races or classes of population of the
    Federation.

    It further states that intent is irrelevant.

    The Act was amended by the Constitution Amendment Act
of 1971 which made it seditious to discuss:

a) citizenship under Article 113;
b) national language and use of other language for non-official purposes under Article 154;
c) quotas for Malays and natives of Borneo and the protection of the legitimate rights of other communities under Article 181;
d) sovereignty of the Ruler.

The implementation of the above can be questioned by the public. But the line between the questioning of the implementation of the above and the seditious discussion of it is thin. Few newspapers have therefore taken up the challenge. There is insufficient precedence in such cases for use by newspapers in determining the line. As a result, newspapers generally play safe and avoid such issues.

Besides the above laws, there are the 'normal' laws covering defamation, obscene literature, pornography, official secrets, etc.

3   TELECOMMUNICATIONS ACTIVITIES

The Telecommunications Department is within the Ministry of Communications. The Department is headed by a Director-General and two Deputies. It is divided into six divisions, each headed by a director: administration and training, development, operations, external services, accounts, and stores and workshop.

The Department is responsible for planning, installing, commissioning and maintaining all broadcast transmitters, as well as the extensive HF and VHF networks for the police, customs, state and municipal fire services, public works department, National Electricity Board, other government departments and quasi-government bodies. It employs 20,000 people with gross assets of M$531.9 million (US$238.3 million) and revenue of M$135.3 million (US$59.6 million) in 1973.

The Department trains its personnel at the Telecommunications Training Centre at Kuala Lumpur. The Centre provides both technical and managerial training. In 1973, there was an expansion in management training for senior officers and supervisory officers of the Department. Eight such courses were conducted. In the same year the Centre also launched its phase IV building project costing M$2.9 millions and adding 30 per cent to training capacity.

Courses at the Centre and its training units at Kota
Kinabalu and Kuching increased from 279 courses and
17,256 trainee-weeks in 1972 to 309 courses and 18,699
trainee-weeks in 1973. Training was also provided for 109
telex operators from the private sector. The two-year
technicians' course conducted by the Centre has been taken
over by the training unit in Kota Kinabalu. The Centre
also organises the departmental examinations, of which
there were 24 in 1973.

Foreign experts have acquainted staff with new crossbar
exchange equipment. New training fields include automatic
telex and computerised message switching, coaxial transmission and troposcatter technology.

The Telecommunications Department provides both inland
and overseas services.

1   Inland services

Inland Telephone Service   There were 198,950 telephones
served by 294 major and rural exchanges and 11 satellite
links in Peninsular Malaysia at the end of 1973. The
number of telephones in Peninsular Malaysia increased
from 98,471 to 198,950 between 1963-73, an annual increase
of 7.3 per cent. Telephones per 1,000 people increased
from 9.8 in 1957 to 18 in 1973.

There were 20,489 new telephone lines installed in
1971, 26,408 in 1972 and 27,451 in 1973. During the same
period, the number of applicants on the waiting lists grew
from 7,440 in 1971 to 10,770 in 1972 to 17,816 in 1973.

The number of subscribers on Subscriber Trunk Dialling
(STD) increased from 94.6 per cent in 1973 to 96 per cent
in 1974. 29,322 new lines were installed in 1974 but the
number of applicants on the waiting list has also grown to
a record 30,156.

Public telephone services are increasing, especially in
the rural areas. In 1963, there were 1,291 public 'phone
booths in Peninsular Malaysia and this increased to
2,285 'phone booths by 1973, excluding 117 'phone booths
in Sabah and Sarawak. More than 60 per cent of these
booths were in the rural areas.

The main exchanges and their capacity are as shown in
Table 1.3.

TABLE 1.3 Total capacity of main exchanges

Main exchange	Total capacity (1974)
Kuala Lumpur	54,200 lines
Penang	13,800 lines
Ipoh	8,200 lines
Malacca	4,000 lines
Johore Bahru	3,900 lines
Seremban	3,300 lines
Kuantan	1,600 lines
Kuala Trengganu	1,100 lines
Kota Baharu	2,000 lines

With the exception of Johore Bahru, STD facilities are available between these main centres. STD is also available from most of these centres to Singapore. The manual exchanges at Teluk Anson and Batu Pahat have been replaced by new automatic crossbar exchanges and provided with STD facilities.

Malaysia is gradually switching over to automatic electronic 'step by step' exchange. New 10,000-line exchanges are now either being installed or are on order.

High capacity microwave systems connect all the main towns of Peninsular Malaysia from Johore Bahru in the south to Penang and Alor Star in the north and Kuantan and Kota Baru on the east coast. VHF and UHF systems are replacing the inferior trunk and junction routes, paving the way for countrywide STD and supplementing the 163 microwave/VHF/UHF stations already in use. Thirty-four additional stations are under construction.

Mobile Radio Telephone Service   Radiophone service is provided for customers to make and receive calls to and from vehicles equipped with suitable radio equipment.

At present this service is only available in Kuala Lumpur and adjoining areas in the state of Selangor. This service will be extended to cover the whole west coast of Peninsular Malaysia.

Inland Telegraph Service   The main telegraph offices are operated by the Telecommunications Department while the Postal Department and the Malayan Railway Administration operate the rest. There were 329 telegraph offices at the end of 1974 in Peninsular Malaysia. Interlinking

of the main telegraph offices is done by voice-frequency
telegraph systems while the smaller offices are served by
the telephone network.

A phonogram service - the dictation of telegrams over
the telephone - is available to all telephone subscribers
and to the general public through public call boxes at all
hours.

Telex is becoming more popular with commercial and
industrial growth.   The service went fully automatic in
April, 1974. With the automatic exchange, subscribers are
now able to key all their inland calls and also international calls to certain countries. Training of teleprinter operators for telex subscribers in Peninsular
Malaysia is carried out by the Telecommunications Training
Centre on request.

2   Overseas service

Overseas Telephone Services   These are available to most
countries. In 1973, they were extended to Bangladesh,
Dubai, Oman, Ras al Khaimah and Sharjah. The services are
provided via cable and satellite circuits and by the end
of 1973 there were 25 cables, 24 satellites and 25 radio
and troposcatter circuits to cater for the telephone traffic which has increased by approximately 35 per cent over
the previous year.

Telex   Telex services are available to 24 countries.
Demand is increasing and the total traffic of 1974 was an
increase of 76 per cent over the previous year. The target is 4,000 lines by 1976. The service is at present fed
by 32 cable, 57 satellite and 20 radio and troposcatter
circuits.

There are also direct telex lines, usually installed by
the larger business organisations. At the end of 1974
there were 40 in use - 20 to Hong Kong, 4 to Thailand, 4
to the United Kingdom, 2 to Australia, 2 to the USA, 1 to
Japan, 6 to Sabah and 1 from Sabah to Singapore.

Phototelegrams and Leased Teleprinter Circuits   The
phototelegraph service is used mainly by the press. The
service is available to Australia, Thailand, South Korea,
United Kingdom, Canada, Germany, Philippines, Hong Kong,
India, Japan, New Zealand, and the USA. Twenty-five private teleprinter circuits were leased by private organisations by the end of 1973.

Telegraph   A telegraph service is available to all
countries and the total telegraph traffic for 1973 showed
an increase of 13.3 per cent over the previous year.
There were 11 cable, 1 satellite and 5 radio and troposcatter circuits by the end of 1973.

3   Telecommunication costs

Telephone Call Charges

Local calls are charged at M$0.10 per call irrespective of
duration.

   Telephonist Controlled Trunk Calls have a minimum charge
which covers the first three minutes of conversation after
which each additional minute is charged at $\frac{1}{3}$ of the three-
minute call charge. A three-minute call from Kuala Lumpur
to Penang, Kota Bharu or Johore Baru would cost M$2.40.

   International Telephone Service has a charge based on
the same principle as that of Telephonist Controlled Trunk
calls. For a three-minute call from Kuala Lumpur to
Manila the cost would be M$22.50. For a similar call to
London the cost would be M$33.00.

   STD Calls' charges are levied in units valued at
M$0.10 for the cost of one local call unit.

   Charges for Telegrams   Within Peninsular Malaysia and
Singapore, the ordinary rate for 10 words or less (including address and signature) is M$1.00. The urgent rate is
double the ordinary rate. Rates for overseas telegrams
may be obtained on application at any telegraph office.
However, as an example, a thirty-word message to Manila
would cost M$30.00 and the same message to Paris would
cost M$42.00.

4   Other services

The Telecommunications Department provides a civil radio
service through an extensive HF and VHF communications
network to various government and quasi-government bodies.
It has a special police service which provides VHF networks for mobile police cars and police stations. The
Department also maintains radio coast stations in Penang,
Kuantan and Kuching to provide services to and from ship-
ping using MF and HF links. A 24-hour watch is kept to

receive urgent signals from ships at sea. Subscribers on
board ship can be connected with the public telephone network through a VHF radio telephone service operated in
Penang and Port Keland.

The short-range (VHF) radiotelephone service provides
communications with ships within 50 miles of Kelang,
Penang and Singapore. The medium range (HF) radiotelephone service is available to ships at sea over sea ranges
of up to 800 miles from Singapore, in the South China Sea,
Malaysian coastal waters and the waters of the Indonesian
Archipelago. Ships at sea anywhere in the world outside
these ranges can be reached through the long range (HP)
radiotelephone service.

The Telecommunications Department provides and maintains
all the communications services between point-to-point,
ground-to-air, and within the airports, on behalf of the
Civil Aviation Department. It also plans, implements and
maintains all the navigational aids throughout the country.

The Department runs a 'leased channel' service to cater
for quasi-governmental and private bodies requiring communication with their mobile vehicles. Businessmen and
government officials use a manual service through the normal operator, but this will be going automatic in 1976.
Taxis, bus companies, and firms like Malaysian Airline
System, Rediffusion, Securicor and Pernas lease channels
via repeaters at Telecommunications Department. Public
services like the police, waterworks and hospitals lease
channels and are given their own repeaters.

The Telecommunications Department mans a frequency
monitoring station, is responsible for the detection and
suppression of radio interference from motor vehicles and
other electrical and industrial equipment and the licensing
of all radio stations and networks.

The number of licences issued in 1973 were as shown in
table 1.4.

The Department is responsible for the allocation and
registration of all radio frequencies and the control of
their transmission. Monthly meetings are held between
Singapore, Brunei and Malaysia to co-ordinate frequency
usage by all civil and military users before registration
with International Telecommunications in Geneva.

TABLE 1.4   Total number of licences issued in 1973

Licences	Total
Radio Citizens' Band (including radio microphone)	254
Radio Station, Amateur	131
Private Radio Communications (VHF, UHF, and HF networks)	
a) private network	104
b) radio telephone linking telephone exchanges	62
c) private network (leased channel)	13
Ship stations (on board a ship not permanently moored)	29
Aircraft stations (a station on board an aircraft)	70
Experimental stations (for experiments in radiocommunication)	33
Press receiving stations (for reception of multi-destination press messages)	4

The Department sets up examinations for ship, radio, telegraph and radio-telephone operators and awards certificates of proficiency to ship radio operators.

The planning, implementation and maintenance of all television transmitting stations in Malaysia is the Telecommunications Department's responsibility. There are 114 radio transmitting stations (ten of which are still under construction) and 23 television transmitting stations (seven still under construction).

5   General information and expansion plans

In the First Malaysian Plan (1965-70), M$50 million (US$22 million) was allocated for telecommunications development. The sum was raised to M$150 million (US$66 million) during the mid-term review of the Plan. The Second Malaysia Plan allocated M$298.39 million (US$131.45 million) for telecommunications' development and this was increased during the mid-term review of the Plan to M$365.83 million (US$161.16 million). It is expected that the Third Malaysia Plan (1975-80) will allocate

M$2,000 million (US$881 million) to the development of telecommunications.

The Department mans Malaysia's earth stations. The first earth station at Kuantan was opened in 1970, using the Indian Ocean Intelsat IV for international telephone calls and occasional live telecasts. A second earth station to allow simultaneous television broadcasts to East Malaysia was on schedule for August 1975. A third station is planned for 1977-8, for international services only.

The Department plans to install at least ten trans- mitting stations over the next decade to handle trunk line calls alone. The capital city, Kuala Lumpur, which at present has 63,000 lines, will have double that number by the end of 1976 and will reach 300,000 by 1980.

4   NATIONAL EDUCATION SYSTEM

Education in Malaysia rests in the hands of the Federal Ministry of Education. The objectives of the Malaysian education system are:

(a)   To strengthen the national education system for unity and solidarity, especially by reducing shortcomings and imbalances so that equal educational opportuni- ties are provided.
(b)   To use Bahasa Malaysia as the main language of instruction.
(c)   To raise the standard of education at all levels through the enhancement of content, the planning of methodology and additional services.
(d)   To give primary importance to science, technology and vocational education.

The number of government schools, i.e. schools that are fully government financed is increasing. Privately-run institutions are also increasing. The number of private candidates sitting for public examinations increased from 47,856 in 1965 to 85,318 in 1973.

The education system in Malaysia consists of five stages: primary, lower secondary or comprehensive, upper secondary or post-comprehensive, post-secondary or sixth form and tertiary (in any of the five local universities).

There are six grades in primary education, with auto- matic promotion. Age of entry is normally six-plus. All

primary schools have common syllabuses and time-tables.
Primary education is provided in the four main languages,
Malay, English, Chinese and Tamil. As from 1970, English
is being replaced as a medium of instruction by Bahasa
Malaysia but will be a compulsory second language in all
schools. Primary education is free.

Children completing six years of primary education are
admitted automatically to the lower secondary stage, which
is comprehensive in character. The aim at this stage is
to offer the child an opportunity to sample various kinds
of studies and to assist in vocational choices.

For three years of comprehensive lower secondary education promotion is automatic. After this, pupils are
selected through a public examination to move to the upper
secondary level for a further two years of education.
Pupils at this level are organised into two groups -
academic and vocational. The academic group is further
organised into three streams - arts, sciences and
technical. The pupils from the academic group finally sit
for the Malaysian Certificate of Education examination and
the vocational group for the Malaysian Vocational Certificate of Education examination.

Pupils who have achieved a good standard in the MCE can
graduate to Form VI, which is divided into three streams -
science, arts and technical. At the end of the second
year, pupils sit another common examination, the Higher
School Certificate, necessary for admission to the five
local universities.

Education in the Malay-medium schools is free while a
nominal monthly fee is charged in the others. Education
accounted for 19 per cent of total government expenditure
in 1960. This proportion increased to 22 per cent in 1974.
The total educational expenditure as a proportion of the
GNP has increased from 3.2 per cent in 1960 to 5.6 per
cent in 1974. The major output indicator, the literacy
rate, has increased from 51 per cent in 1957 to 68 per
cent in 1970.

The proportion of the population remaining in school has
also increased; as shown in table 1.5.

The government is trying to increase the number of students in technical and vocational schools. Enrolment in
such schools increased from 1,566 to 10,159 between 1965
and 1973. To increase the proportion of science students

TABLE 1.5   Proportion of population remaining in school

Age	1957	1973
6 - 11	80%	91%
12 - 14	15%	60%
15 - 16	11%	25%

from the rural background, nine special science secondary schools have been established in West Malaysia. The intake for these schools in 1973 was 9,243. Enrolment in science is increasing. The ratio between arts and science enrolment in 1971 was 66:34 and in 1974 was 52:48.

The national teacher-pupil ratio has remained stable at 1:30 since 1970.

Higher Learning Institutions   There are three colleges and five universities in Malaysia. Together, their enrolment was expected to reach 29,030 by 1975. This would represent an increase of 118 per cent over the enrolment of 1970 which was 13,324.

The Ungku Omar Polytechnic in Ipoh, Perak was expected to have about 1,300 students in 1975. New courses are to be introduced including a course in marine engineering designed to meet increasing demand for marine engineers.

The Institute of Technology, MARA (ITM) was established to train Malay professional and sub-professional manpower. Student enrolment in 1975 was about 6,000. The college offers courses at the mid-management level, including accountancy, administration and law, applied science, architecture, business management, engineering, hotel and catering management and library science.

The Tunku Abdul Rahman College is a private institution receiving government financial support. The courses offered range from pre-university to the professional and sub-professional levels. At the professional level, the College trains students in accountancy, chartered secretaryship, building technology, mathematics and biological and physical sciences. Enrolment was expected to be 3,000 by 1975. New courses in automobile engineering and electronics will be introduced. A new campus at Ulu Klang in Selangor was expected to be completed by mid-1975, for which the government has allocated M$8.5 million.

The University of Malaya is the largest institution of higher learning in Malaysia, and was established in 1962. Enrolment was expected to reach 8,600 in 1975. The faculties at present consist of Agriculture, Arts, Economics and Administration, Education, Engineering, Medicine, Science, Dentistry, and Law. The University confers over 3,000 degrees and diplomas yearly.

The National University, established in 1970, is the first university to use Bahasa Malaysia as its medium of instruction. It planned to have 2,647 students by 1975. It will be relocated at Bangi-Selangor in 1976. It has five faculties: Arts, Islamic Studies, Science, Economics and Management, Medicine. An Institute of Malay Language, Literature and Culture has also been established. Its permanent campus at Bangi is intended to accommodate 10,000 students.

The University of Science, Malaysia (USM) established in 1969, was expected to have a student population of 2,685 by 1975. The university has no faculties, but is based on a system of schools. It offers courses in the basic sciences, pharmacy, education, housing and planning technology, the social sciences and the humanities. The University of Science also conducts off-campus courses. It is the only university offering a degree course in Mass Communications. Medical, nursing and military science courses are planned.

The University of Agriculture was established in 1971 as a result of a merger between the College of Agriculture and the Faculty of Agriculture at the University of Malaya. Total enrolment at the University of Agriculture was expected to reach 2,375 in 1975. The first batch of 114 students for the degree course in agriculture, forestry, veterinary medicine and animal science was admitted in 1973.

The National Institute of Technology, formerly known as the Technical College, was elevated to university status in 1972 offering a two-tier programme at diploma and degree levels. It was expected to have 2,450 students by 1975. The new degree programme at the Institute offers courses in mechanical, civil and electrical engineering architecture.

Educational broadcasting

Radio broadcasts to schools began in the late 1940s under

the control of Radio Singapore, which received about
M$300,000 annually from the states of Malaya towards the
service.   In 1959, two years after independence, the service moved to Kuala Lumpur.

In May 1966 schools radio broadcasting became part of
a new Schools Broadcasting Service under the Ministry of
Education.   In 1972 the organisation for educational broadcasting was further developed with the creation of the
Educational Media Service as a division of the Education
Ministry.   This coincided with the creation of an educational television service and the EMS division now has
three components: the Schools Radio Service, ETV and the
Audio-Visual Aids Unit (AVA).

The EMS Division's main functions are:
(a)   planning and production of radio and TV programmes
      to schools;
(b)   planning, production and distribution of AVA materials
      to schools and institutions;
(c)   equipping and organising a film library, service and
      loan of educational films, film scripts and AVA
      materials to schools and other institutions; and
(d)   training of teachers in media use and evaluation.
      including operation and maintenance of audio-visual
      equipment.

The Schools Radio service broadcasts in four languages - Bahasa Malaysia, English, Chinese, and Tamil -
for pupils from Standard 1 to Form 6.

Educational television began on June 19, 1972, based
on the experience gained in two pilot projects in 1965 and
1966.   The evaluation report of the pilot projects recommended that:
The Malaysian Government is in the position to benefit
directly and immediately from the establishment of an
Educational Television Service.   While the schools
would make the initial and more obvious demands on the
hours available for transmission, the potential for
related applications in industry, agriculture and rural
and health development programmes appears limitless and
would encourage the expansion of the service (Alan
Hancock, 'The Development of Educational Mass Media in
Malaysia').

The report also recommended that television in schools
be designed to meet some of the demands of the Malaysian
educational system, such as:

(a)   the need to bring supplementary instructional resour-
      ces to the classroom, thus enabling the teacher to
      provide the best possible lessons;
(b)   the need to provide instruction in specialised areas
      where there is a lack of qualified teachers;
(c)   the need to accommodate a rapidly increasing enrol-
      ment, coupled with the inability to provide sufficient
      numbers of trained staff;
(d)   the need to provide in-service training for unquali-
      fied teachers in subject matter and methods;
(e)   the need to improve the structure and content of the
      school curriculum to comply with the demands of
      society and to ensure a uniform quality in urban and
      rural areas;
(f)   the need to provide in-service training of all
      teachers prior to the implementation of new curricula.

Chapter 2

DEVELOPMENT OF BROADCASTING: HISTORICAL PERSPECTIVE

1 RADIO

Broadcasting in Malaya before the Second World War was conducted on an amateur basis. In those days, a small radio station provided a limited service to Kuala Lumpur under the then United Kingdom Ministry of Information and Propaganda.

In 1942, Malaya was occupied by the Japanese who added small stations at Penang, Malacca and Seremban. With the end of the war in 1946, the Department of Broadcasting was created, known as Radio Malaya. It was administered from Singapore, and started with a small staff and ex-service equipment.

However, it was the 12-year Emergency in Malaya which resulted in the rapid expansion of the Broadcasting Department. (The Emergency started with the outbreak of militant communist terrorism in 1948.) Particularly between the years 1950-55, staff recruitment to technical facilities progressively expanded and improved.

On 1 January 1959, a new radio service was inaugurated in Kuala Lumpur after Malaya achieved Independence in August 1957. This new service was designed solely to serve the federation. Since then, broadcasting has expanded at all levels including radio services in East Malaysia when Sabah and Sarawak joined the federation. In 1963, the Overseas Service was established with broadcasts in Indonesian, English and Mandarin and the station call of 'Suara Malaysia' ('Voice of Malaysia'). With the formation of Malaysia on 16 September 1963, Radio Malaya became Radio Malaysia.

From 1963, regional broadcast stations were set up all over the country, first in Kota Bharu.

After operating at Federal House for 15 years Radio Malaysia began broadcasting on 9 May 1972 from the new Radio House (Wisma Radio) in Angkasapuri, now the biggest broadcasting complex in South East Asia. A six-storey technical and administration building, the Wisma Radio facilities include two auditoria (seating 1,000 and 250 people), 21 studios and full technical facilities.

Despite the introduction of television in 1963, radio still has a large audience, especially among the rural people. While other means of communication failed to penetrate remoter areas, radio succeeded cheaply and efficiently. For many, radio was the prime source of information and entertainment.

By 1973, with the rapid expansion of Kuala Lumpur as a business and administration centre, Radio Malaysia Ibukota was started as a pilot service for the population within a 20-30 mile radius of the city centre. Programmes can be heard on 250 metres medium wave and provide entertainment, local news, traffic guidance and general information.

In June 1975, Radio Malaysia introduced a FM stereo service.

TABLE 2.1 Significant landmarks and events in the development of radio

Date		Event
	1921	First radio set in Malaysia.
	1928	Malayan Wireless Society formed in Kuala Lumpur.
	1930	Malayan Wireless Society began thrice-weekly transmissions on 325 metres from Petaling Hill, Kuala Lumpur.
	1934	Penang Wireless Society (Station ZHJ) began transmissions in Malay, Chinese, Tamil and English on 49.3 metres.
1 Mar.	1937	Official opening of British Malaya Broadcasting Corporation studios and transmitters at Caldecott Hill, Singapore.

Date	Event
1940	British Malaya Broadcasting Corporation taken over by Government of the Straits Settlements.
1940-1941	First Malayan overseas broadcasts begun by Station ZHJ in Penang in Thai language.
Aug. 1942-1945	Broadcasting came under control of Japanese. Broadcasts from Penang, Kuala Lumpur, Seremban, Malacca and Singapore.
Sep. 1945	British Military Administration took over broadcasting.
1 Apr. 1946	Department of Broadcasting set up with headquarters in Singapore.
18 June 1948	Emergency declared throughout Federation of Malaya.
1951	Radio Malaya began Emergency and Rurual Broadcasts.
7 June 1954	Radio Sarawak officially inaugurated.
Nov. 1955	Radio Sabah officially inaugurated.
1956	Radio Malaya's Kuala Lumpur station moved to Federal House from Jalan Young.
31 Aug. 1957	Merdeka (Independence).
1 Jan. 1959	Singapore station separated and Radio Malaya moved to Kuala Lumpur.
1 Jan. 1962	Radio Malaya began commercial broadcasts.
15 Feb. 1963	The Overseas Service or The Voice of Malaya established with broadcasts in Indonesian, English and Mandarin.
16 Sep. 1963	Proclamation of Malaysia. Radio Malaysia came into existence and the Voice of Malaya became The Voice of Malaysia.
16 Nov. 1963	First regional broadcast begun by Radio Malaysia in Kota Bharu.
15 Mar. 1965	Ipoh transmitting station operational
Apr. 1965	First FM broadcast in Malaysia from Mt Kinabulu station, Sabah.

Date	Event
2 May 1966	Radio Malaysia started Schools' Broadcast Service for primary schools in Peninsular Malaysia.
May 1966	Kuala Trengganu transmitting station operational.
June 1966	Radio Malaysia, Johore Bharu, officially opened.
June 1966	Kuantan transmitting station operational.
11 Oct. 1969	Radio Malaysia and Television Malaysia integrated to become the Department of Broadcasting, Malaysia.
1 Apr. 1971	Silver Jubilee of Department of Broadcasting.
19 Apr. 1972	Radio Malaysia's National Network began 24-hour broadcasts.
9 May 1972	Radio Malaysia began broadcasts from Wisma Radio in the Angkasapuri complex.
1 Nov. 1972	The Voice of Malaysia began broadcasts in Arabic.
1 Jan. 1973	The Schools' Broadcast Service taken over by the Ministry of Education.
1 Oct. 1973	The Voice of Malaysia began broadcasts in Tagalog.
5 Nov. 1973	Radio Malaysia Siaran Ibukota launched.
June 1975	FM stereo service was introduced.

2   TELEVISION

Television began on 28 December 1963, with one network operating from temporary studios at the Dewan Tunku Abdul Rahman, Kuala Lumpur.   In October 1969 it moved to Angkasapuri.

Government advisors for the pilot television service came mainly from the Canadian Broadcasting Corporation.

Television Malaysia started with 24 hours of air time per week, which was increased to 44 hours.   A second channel was added on 17 November 1969.

The installation of a series of microwave links from

Johore (in the south) to Kedah (in the north) has led to
the rapid expansion of television coverage on the entire
west coast. These installations have also helped introduce a pilot service in the east-coast state of Kelantan.

Until 1969 there were 11 transmitting stations. At
present, there are 23 transmitters in 16 locations within
the country's microwave system, operated by the Department
of Telecommunications.

Educational television for primary and secondary
schools began in June 1972. By 1974 the annual total of
ETV programmes broadcast was 1,368 hours.

Malaysia's first earth satellite communication station
was opened in Kuantan, Pahang in 1970. This M$9 million
station uses the Indian Ocean Intelsat IV for international telephone calls and occasional live telecasts.
A second earth station to allow simultaneous television
broadcasts to East Malaysia was on schedule for August
1975. This may use Intelsat IV or another of the Intelsat
series over the Pacific. Yet another satellite station,
for international services only, is planned for 1977-8.

Malaysia had hoped to introduce colour television in
1975, but for economic and technical reasons, the deci-
sion was postponed, perhaps for 1976. Conversion to
colour is estimated to cost between M$60-100 million over
seven to eight years. The four television studios are
now being changed, and all the new equipment acquired
by Television Malaysia is colour compatible. Transmitters
installed when television was introduced in 1963 will have
to be changed completely; more recent ones can be adapted.

TABLE 2.2 Significant landmarks and events in the
development of television

Date	Event
16 Mar. 1960	The Cabinet appointed subcommittee to examine possibility of a television service.
28 Dec. 1963	Television began over one network, at the Dewan Tunku Abdul Rahman, Kuala Lumpur.
20 Apr. 1964	Installation of two transmitters at Gunung Keledang to Gunung Tampin, giving coverage to Lumut in the north, Malacca and surround-ing areas in the south.

Date	Event
1964	Television was providing 50 per cent live programmes, 4 language newscasts (English, Malay, Chinese and Indian), and a nightly world news roundup.
15 May 1964	Kuala Lumpur transmitters increased power from 10 KW to 100 KW Effective Radiated Power (ERP).
1 Oct. 1964	Kedah Peak television station on Gunung Jerai opened to feed northern states of Peninsular Malaysia.
28 Dec. 1964	Television made a permanent service.
April 1965	Four new transmitters installed at Johore Bharu, Batu Pahat, Kluang and Taiping, thus including entire west coast of Peninsular Malaysia within the national network.
30 July 1966	Television network extended to Kota Bharu area in Kelantan.
3 Dec. 1966	M$4 million microwave scheme initiated to link the 3 east coast capitals of Kuantan, Kota Bharu and Kuala Trengganu.
11 Oct. 1969	Radio Malaysia and Television Malaysia integrated as Department of Broadcasting.
6 Nov. 1969	Department of Television moved to Angkasa-puri, a 33-acre site at Bukit Putra, Pantai Valley, Kuala Lumpur.
17 Nov. 1969	Second TV channel launched.
1970	Malaysia's first earth satellite station opened in Kuantan, Pahang.
19 June 1972	Educational Television launched by Prime Minister Tun Abdul Razak bin Datuk Hussein.

Chapter 3

REGULATIONS AND POLICIES FOR BROADCASTING OPERATIONS

1 GENERAL OBJECTIVES AND GOALS

A distinction must be made between the Department of
Broadcasting (RTM) on one hand and Radio RAAF (Royal
Australian Air Force) and Rediffusion on the other. Radio
RAAF is allowed to operate solely because of the
Australian air-base at Butterworth. It is for the entertainment of RAAF personnel, covers less than a ten-mile
radius and operates under a special charter. Rediffusion
is a commercial wired-service, operating under conditions
stipulated in a licence, and is only meant to provide
entertainment programmes. In this description of general
objectives and goals for broadcasting in Malaysia,
Radio RAAF and Rediffusion are excluded.

RTM, being a government department, is primarily concerned with serving the government and the nation's
needs. Its objectives are incorporated within guidelines
laid down by the Ministry of Information to all government communicators and broadcasters.

2 LEGAL RELATIONSHIPS

The Department of Broadcasting (RTM) is headed by a
Director-General responsible to the Minister of Information. The Minister of Information is responsible to
Parliament. All main broadcasting policies are formulated at Cabinet level. The Ministry of Information
administers and executes agreed policies which are out-
lined once a year in the King's Speech and which can be
debated, if necessary, by Parliament. In addition, the
Minister of Information usually reports to Parliament
three times a year on actions or proposed actions of the
Ministry of Information.

3   POLICIES ON ADVISORY BOARD

Within the Ministry of Information, there is a Planning
Council whose chairman is either the Minister, or his
alternate, the Deputy Minister, of Information. This
Planning Council usually meets every Monday, Wednesday
and Friday and is attended by all divisional heads,
including those in the Department of Broadcasting. This
Planning Council meeting determines day-to-day strategy
of implementing the policies and deals with important
issues of the day. The Council's main function is to
guide or advise on the communication strategy in imparting
information to the people.

There is also a Parliamentary Committee on Mass Media
which has representatives from other Ministries and co-
ordinates communication activities supporting government
programmes. Since a lot of co-ordination and integration
approaches are needed, the Ministry of Information
attaches a liaison officer to each Ministry.

4   TRANSMISSION POLICIES

There is no policy determining the physical extent of
broadcasts but the extent may be influenced by political
considerations. The distribution of transmitters and
their power is determined by the following factors:
(a)   population density;
(b)   cost per head considerations: the lower the cost per
      head, the stronger the transmitter;
(c)   purpose and urgency: in areas where there is the
      possibility of a threat to national security, the
      transmitter will be stronger to reach as many people
      as possible, even if the cost per head is high;
(d)   development purposes.

There is no policy determining duration of broadcasts.
Cost is the main consideration plus accessibility of the
audience. The National Network of Radio Malaysia broadcasts for 24 hours and the original reason was to reach
fishermen, drivers, etc. who work in the night. There is
no policy determining the allocation of air time for each
particular type of programme. The present proportion of
the different types of programmes in RTM was reached after
an attempt to strike a balance. There is a standing
policy now that there should be more development orientated programmes.

5   COVERAGE POLICIES

Political

Private broadcasting stations are banned from political broadcasting. Political coverage is only allowed on RTM during national elections: the air time given is dependent on the number of House of Representatives' seats contested by each political party.

Commercial

There is no policy determining the extent of commercial broadcasting but RTM does not allow commercial breaks in individual programmes. Commercials must be vetted by a committee in the Ministry of Information for 'good taste' and 'Made-in-Malaysia' requirements, and by the National Censorship Board. There is a 50 per cent surcharge for each showing of imported advertisements.

   Commercials are expected to conform to the regulations set by the Advertising Standards Authority Malaysia (ASAM) and the Copy Code of the Commercial Division, Ministry of Information. Generally, advertisements must be Malaysian in character, sincere and must not contravene the laws of the country. Advertisements must also take into consideration the Islamic religious laws (no advertising of foods with pork content, etc.).

Public services

No policy regulates the use of air time for public-service broadcasts. Broadcasting agencies are encouraged to provide such services voluntarily. RTM will provide such services when approached by individual organisations. Discretion, however, lies with RTM. RTM's priority concerning public-service announcements is national and community interest. There is no charge for such announcements.

Air time

No policy regulates the availability of air time for commercial broadcasting in private broadcasting stations. RTM, being a government department, cannot use air time for commercial purposes at the expense of the other programmes. Rates of commercials broadcast over RTM are determined by the Commercial Division, Ministry of Information. Political air time over Radio Malaysia is provided free of charge.

6   POLICIES ON CONTENT OF PROGRAMMES

News

Local news gets more coverage and air time than foreign. Preference in local news is given to news that is development orientated, and which promotes the government image and government policies. Very little in-depth political news is allowed over RTM. Political news is limited to election results and reporting of such hard facts. Political disagreement between politicians or political parties is not revealed. News items are also governed by Islamic religious laws.

The average ratio of local to foreign news is 60:40, but this is just a guideline. Priority in foreign news is dependent on its importance and its relevance to Malaysia such as news about the Asean (Association of South East Asian Nations) countries, South East Asian affairs, Asia/Middle-East and the rest of the world, in that order; foreign news stories promoting religious fraternity and those touching on the economy of the country.

The major foreign news sources are Reuters, Associated Press, Agence France Presse (AFP), UPI, and Antara, and news from foreign stations monitored at Kelang.

All stations must broadcast at least 2½ hours of news daily from RTM.

Information/documentaries

The emphasis of most information programmes and document- aries is on development and civic consciousness, and current government campaigns, with overriding emphasis still on the New Economic Policy and the Rukunegara.

There is no limit on the number of foreign informa- tional documentaries that can be imported, except that they cannot exceed 40 per cent of overall programming. Imported documentaries that are instructional, educational

and informative are given highest preference. Documentaries for children are also given preference. Documentaries that are not political or religious and are cul-
turally agreeable are normally acceptable. Any document-
ary from the United Nations or its associated bodies will
be accepted. Documentaries from Deutsche Welle are most
popular with RTM at present.

Entertainment and drama

All Malaysian dramas broadcast must depict the multi-
racial nature of Malaysian society and must reflect
Malaysian identity. Ideas broadcast must not be
'foreign' to Malaysian society and must not contravene
the laws.

   The hair length and appearance of television performers
is taken into consideration. Songs that are 'too wild'
are not encouraged but songs of all languages are broadcast over the four different radio networks and this is
one of the ways considered helpful in eradicating the
association of different languages with different networks, and in promoting national unity. (Radio channels
which were formerly divided into English, Bahasa Malaysia,
Chinese and Tamil are now distinguished by colour codes.)

   Entertainment and drama programmes are now also
development orientated and are expected to convey the
principles of the Rukunegara. Entertainment is considered a vehicle for cultural development and attempts are
being made to develop a national culture. Foreign feature films still form a high percentage of entertainment
programmes, but attempts are being made to produce more
local comedy, musical and variety programmes.

Commercials

There is no restriction on the number of advertisements
broadcast each week. The limiting factor in RTM's case
is the availability of air time.

   Advertisements using subliminal techniques are banned,
as are those with religious, political or racial themes.
All advertisements over Network One of Television Malaysia
must be in Bahasa Malaysia. Foreign advertisements should
not carry messages or depict scenes that are offensive to
Malaysian society.

Advertisements that have scenes or messages offensive to Muslims are not allowed over Network One of Television Malaysia. The more important policies pertaining to the content of commercials include:

(a)   no product claiming to treat any condition which properly requires professional medical attention is allowed;

(b)   no advertisement that tends to endanger health or character; or to offend the proprieties or ethics generally observed by the community is allowed;

(c)   no advertisement attempting to exploit any abnormal national or international events or conditions is allowed;

(d)   no advertisement making irreverent reference to any name, incident or concept of religious significance is allowed;

(e)   no advertisement containing statements, scenes or suggestions which may offend the religious, racial, political or sentimental susceptibilities of any section of the community is allowed;

(f)   no advertisement is allowed if it tends to subvert or disparage law and order, adult authority or moral standards;

(g)   no advertisement is allowed if it contains scenes of drinking alcohol if such material is meant for Network One;

(h)   no advertisement is allowed if it has scenes of lip-to-lip kissing or long-haired men;

(i)   no advertisement is allowed if it contains scenes showing pork or pork products;

(j)   no advertisement is allowed if it contains terms, words, scenes or subject matter not generally considered acceptable in polite company;

(k)   no advertisement is allowed if it publicises meetings of a political or a religious nature.
(More details of the above are in the Copy Rules of the Commercial Division, Ministry of Information.)

Public services

Broadcasting agencies are not obliged to broadcast public services announcements from the government. All public service announcements over Network One of Television Malaysia or the National Network of Radio Malaysia must be in Bahasa Malaysia.

7   POLICIES ON EDUCATIONAL BROADCASTING

The policies on educational broadcasting in Malaysia are incorporated in the objectives of the Malaysian Education System and the objectives of the Educational Media Service.

There is no provision for the establishment of private educational broadcasting stations. If such a station was permitted the operating conditions would be stated in the licence, imposed by the Minister of Information.

Government policy is to have Bahasa Malaysia as the sole language of instruction for all levels of education by 1983, so Educational Media Services (EMS) is gradually introducing more programmes in the national language. All broadcasts for primary schools are already in Bahasa Malaysia. Programmes are expected to complement the national curriculum and the emphasis is on the teaching of science and technology. Lately, citizenship training and civics have gained importance. Educational programmes are also expected to bear in mind the multi-racial nature of Malaysian society and no racial stereotyping, criticism of religion or similar issues is allowed. Policies on subject areas and types of presentation are normally formulated by the Advisory Committee to the EMS.

No policy stipulates the objectives in the use of radio for educational broadcasting as distinct from the use of television for educational broadcasting. Each is expected to cover the areas it is best suited for. Therefore, ETV has a high percentage of science and mathematics programmes while School Radio has none. The emphasis, however, would seem to be on the expansion of ETV.

8   OFFICIAL/FORMAL CONTROL MECHANISMS

All broadcasting stations must abide by the laws of the country. As well as those described above, there are the Radio and Telecommunications Regulations, which stipulate the conditions under which a broadcast station may operate. Licences for stations cost M$100 a year, can be in any form deemed fit by the Minister of Information and may be issued for any period at the discretion of the Minister. The regulations for programming will be incorporated in the licence. An example is the requirement for both Radio RAAF and Rediffusion to relay at least two hours of news broadcasts from RTM daily.

Broadcasting stations in Malaysia, especially RTM, practice a high degree of self-censorship. The ABU (Asian Broadcasting Union) code is another voluntary control mechanism that RTM adheres to. The Davao Code on conflict reporting is also practised by some of the news editors in RTM.

The government has full authority to use RTM air time as RTM is a government department. The conditions under which the government may make use of the air time of private broadcasting stations are spelt out under the licences to operate, the details of which are confidential.

9   FINANCING POLICIES

As part of the Ministry of Information, RTM is funded through the Government Treasury. An allocation is given to cover all expenditure, including development expenditure. RTM is not allowed to receive any funds directly from other bodies. All loans and such financial aids from other bodies are channelled through the Treasury. Non-governmental broadcasting agencies do not receive financial aid from the government. These agencies can receive financial aid from outside bodies directly.

The amount allocated to RTM is decided by the Treasury after meetings between Treasury and RTM officials. Approval of additional allocation will depend on the needs of the moment, national interest and political considerations. A case in point is the plan to link, via satellite, East Malaysia and Peninsular Malaysia to permit simultaneous television coverage. Political considerations and national interest override the cost factor. The Minister of Information can approach the Minister of Finance directly if there is any sudden financial requirements. He also has access to the Prime Minister for additional allocations if all other channels fail.

No policy stipulates the ways a broadcasting agency may use to derive income. But RTM, being a government agency, can only derive income from licensing and advertisements. To do otherwise would be defeating its objectives and goals. Advertising income to broadcasting agencies is not limited except in the case of RTM. Its availability of air time for commercial purposes is limited, since its priority is to inform and educate the public.

At the moment, only wired broadcasting agencies are

given licences to operate privately with the exception of
Radio RAAF which is the only non-government broadcasting
agency allowed to transmit over the air. Applications for
a licence to operate a broadcasting agency have to be made
to the Telecommunications Department and the Ministry of
Information the final approvals of which have to go
through the Cabinet. Rediffusion, the only privately
owned broadcasting agency, pays about M$30,000 annually to
the government as licence fees.

All broadcasting agencies, including RTM and Educational Media Service, have to pay the Telecommunications
Department for the use of cables and/or transmitters. The
rates are not available, but RTM pays about M$4 million
annually to the Telecommunications Department.

Department of Broadcasting expenditure is audited by
the Treasury. The expenditure/income of non-government
broadcasting agencies does not have to be audited by the
government.

10   CO-ORDINATION POLICIES

There is no formal requirement for broadcasting agencies
to co-ordinate with each other. There have, however, been
a number of informal meetings between RTM and Rediffusion
officials to co-ordinate campaigns initiated by the
government. RTM headquarters in Kuala Lumpur co-ordinates
and decides most matters for the regional stations; in
reality this amounts to a delegation of activities.

11   OPERATIONAL RELATIONSHIPS BETWEEN BROADCASTING
AGENCIES AND OTHER BODIES

RTM depends on the Public Service Commission (a non-
governmental body directly responsible to the King) for
recruitment and promotion of staff and on the Public
Service Department for staff discipline, salary and such
staff matters. On policy matters, RTM depends on the
Ministry of Home Affairs, Ministry of Foreign Affairs and
the National Security Council. An example is the formation of an advisory committee - the Suara Malaysia Wisma
Putra committee - with representatives from the Ministries
of Foreign Affairs and Information, to provide policy
guidelines for RTM's overseas service.

The transmission of RTM programmes largely depends on

the Telecommunications Department and is mainly on a commercial basis.   Rediffusion has no relationship with the
Telecommunications Department as it has its own cable network.   Radio RAAF has its own transmitters.   RTM liaises
with the Telecommunications Department on the purchase and
choosing of sites for new transmitters.

Regional stations have an informal relationship with
state governments and local authorities, providing extensive services to them, as long as there is no conflict
with federal policies.   The regional stations are under
federal jurisdiction.   State governments do not have any
jurisdiction whatsoever over the regional stations.

There are statutory relationships between broadcasting
agencies and no national or local bodies but the National
Security Council and the Ministry of Home Affairs dictate
policies to the broadcasting agencies, including RTM.

Broadcasting agencies are expected to co-operate with
bodies like the police and the army in matters of national
interest.   The discretion lies with the broadcasting
agencies.

12   MANAGERIAL RECRUITMENT POLICIES

Management personnel are chosen by the Public Service
Commission (PSC).   Vacancies are normally advertised in
national newspapers and the government gazette; candidates are interviewed by the PSC, screened for police
records, and then selected.   In other cases, vacancies
are filled by promotion.

Management personnel of the Department of Broadcasting
are responsible to the Director-General of Broadcasting,
the Secretary-General of the Ministry, the Deputy-Minister,
and ultimately, to the Minister of Information himself.
Management positions are permanent and pensionable.

Recruitment is based on experience in the relevant
field, educational qualification and the Bumiputra quota
(a government policy which stipulates that a certain percentage of jobs in an organisation should be reserved for
the indigenous people of Malaysia, i.e. the Malays, Ibans,
etc.).   Other factors are the candidate's personal integ-
rity, leadership qualities and commitment to national
goals.

The managerial recruitment policies of the government do not affect private broadcasting agencies.

13   POLICIES ON EMPLOYMENT PROCEDURES

There is no policy prohibiting the staff of broadcasting agencies from forming a national union, but no such union exists at present. The staff of the Department of Broadcasting are members of the National Union of Employees in Public and Civil Services.

In all private broadcast companies, at least 40 per cent of the work force should be Bumiputras and the racial composition should reflect the racial composition of the country. In government departments, no such policy applies as the majority of the work force is expected to be Bumiputras.

There is a policy of Malaysianisation in private companies. Non-Malaysians need work-permits and are hired on contract. The maximum work-permit period is normally three years, after which it can be renewed.

The Department of Broadcasting normally advertises non-managerial and executive staff vacancies in national newspapers. An interview board consisting of representatives from the Department, the Public Services Commission and the Public Services Department interviews and selects the candidates. This same procedure is used occasionally for approving promotions.

14   POLICIES ON INTERNATIONAL LOANS/AIDS

All international assistance to any government ministry or department must be channelled through the Economic Planning Unit. In general, the government welcomes international assistance as long as the conditions of the assistance can be mutually agreed upon by the donor agency and recipient organisations. A high degree of flexibility and self-determination should be given to the recipient organisations to carry out their programmes, which should be based on national priorities and needs.

The Department of Broadcasting has received international aid mainly as technical assistance. From 1973-5, RTM had, among others:

```
1              technical advisor for research (BBC)
1              engineering advisor (BBC)
4              Peace Corps volunteers attached to the NBTC
               (National Broadcasting Training Centre)
1              UNDP (United Nations Development Programme)
               expert attached to NBTC
```

RTM has also sent a number of employees for training abroad funded by Japan and the Colombo Plan.

15 REGULATIONS AND FOREIGN IMPORTS

Advertisements

There is a 50 per cent surcharge on current rates for every showing of foreign-made advertisement films. The surcharge came into effect on 1 January 1973 as a result of a government policy to assist the local film industry.

To be exempted from the 50 per cent surcharge, an advertisement must be officially passed by the Guild of Advertising Film Producers and bear a Made-in-Malaysia certificate. A Made-in-Malaysia film must fulfill the following conditions:
(a) all artists must be Malaysian (Caucasian-looking artists must get prior approval);
(b) no scenes or shots that can be done in Malaysia are shot overseas;
(c) all technical and creative staff must be Malaysians or expatriates paying Malaysia income tax;
(d) no more than 30 per cent of the total footage of the film can be made outside Malaysia.

Agencies must get a permit from the Customs Department to import advertisements and then, prior to public screening, the approval of the National Censorship Board in the Ministry of Home Affairs.

Programmes

Comedies and thrillers are popular. There is a trend to import programmes from the Third World, but the biggest suppliers are still the USA and Europe. The Film Supply Service, under the charge of a Film Procurement Officer, is responsible for all syndicated and features films screened by Television Malaysia.

Censorship

All foreign and local productions are subjected to censorship by the National Censorship Board. Advertisements and
films are censored if they are considered to be offensive
to public morality and decency, encouraging criminal
offences, portraying racialism either explicitly or
implicitly, expressing extremism, fanaticism, criticism
and cynicism or disrespect for any religion, or portraying
communist ideology either explicitly or implicitly.
Advertisements and films of excessive violence are similarly subjected to censorship. Films with horror themes
are classed for adults only. RTM has a branch of the
National Censorship Board in its headquarters in Kuala
Lumpur.

Physical facilities

No information is available on policies regarding the
import of physical facilities. At present, most of the
equipment in RTM is imported, mainly from Japan.

16   POLICIES ON TRAINING

Training of RTM broadcasting personnel takes place at the
National Broadcasting Training Centre (NBTC), which is
supervised by the National Broadcasting Training Committee,
headed by the Director-General, Department of Broadcasting.
On this committee are the Directors of Programmes, News,
Engineering, Public Affairs and Training Divisions of the
Department, the Deputy Director-General and a representa-
tive from the Ministry of Information. The Director of
NBTC is the Secretary of the National Committee.

Part of the National Committee's task is to determine
the training policies, which may be summarised as follows:
(a)   to train staff in basic skills so as to equip them to
      be proficient in their trade and to attain a minimum
      professional standard;
(b)   to train staff so that the Department of Broadcasting
      can make full use of their capabilities;
(c)   to provide staff with a comprehensive training pro-
      gramme to develop their careers and better their
      prospects;
(d)   to train staff in relation to the role of broadcast-
      ing as a medium of communication which can assist the
      government in its overall developmental efforts or
      undertakings.

Overseas training is provided when the need arises and also where the training cannot be provided by NBTC. There are no policies about overseas training. Priorities depend on the needs of the moment, the funds available and whether or not the personnel can be released.

There are no specific requirements for the setting up of training programmes by any broadcasting agency in the country. There are also no policies about training in private broadcasting networks.

17 POLICIES ON RESEARCH

There is no definite policy on research. At RTM, non-engineering research is undertaken by a research section in the Ministry of Information while engineering research is presently undertaken by the Design and Development Section of the Engineering Division in the Department of Broadcasting. A Research Centre for engineering and applied research is planned.

RTM also commissions commercial companies for research on radio and television audiences. Other broadcasting agencies can conduct their own research activities. Universities and other research agencies are also encouraged to conduct research on communication.

Chapter 4

ORGANISATION AND PROCESSES OF THE DEPARTMENT OF BROADCASTING (RTM)

1 OBJECTIVES AND GOALS

Television Malaysia

As a government medium, the objectives and goals of
Television Malaysia are in line with those of the Ministry
of Information:
(a) to integrate government programmes and policies and
     filter them down to the masses;
(b) to promote national unity;
(c) to stimulate public opinions and interest through
     interesting programmes;
(d) to develop civic consciousness;
(e) to provide information and entertainment.

   Although television is fairly new in Malaysia, celebra-
ting its first decade in 1973, it has become an important
means of helping to change people's attitudes, and works
towards helping them to be development-orientated in line
with government's aims. Entertainment, which accounts for
at least half of the air time, is considered 'the sugar
coating on the pill'.

Radio Malaysia

Audience research has found that television, cinema and
newspapers are chiefly urban-based and do not penetrate
the language and literacy barriers as well as radio.

   There are several programme series solely on rural
development which are produced under the guidance of an
Advisory Committee with representatives from all departments of the Ministry of Agriculture and Co-operatives,

47

Ministry of Rural Development, Majlis Amanah Rakyat or
MARA (Council of Trust for the Indigenous People), Rubber
Research Institute and several other organisations.

Besides providing entertainment, radio attempts to
raise the standards of Malaysian arts and culture simul-
taneously through listeners' participation in competitions,
interviews and speeches, etc.

2   COVERAGE

Television Malaysia

Television can now be received in most parts of Peninsular
Malaysia through 23 transmitting stations (seven still
under construction).   Plans are being drawn up for an
additional transmitting station at Jerantut, in the state
of Pahang.   The physical radius and power of each station
can be found in the Appendix.

The programmes of TV Malaysia, categorised under News,
Drama, Information and Education, and Entertainment, are
intended for nationwide audience broadcast over two chan-
nels - Network I and Network II.   Network I serves as the
National Network whereby all announcements, advertise-
ments, openings and closings are in Bahasa Malaysia.
Network II permits advertisements in other languages like
English, Chinese and Indian.

Daily air time for Network I averages nine hours, and
for Network II, five hours.   However, an extra two to
three hours are added to Network I during weekends.   Network I carries more programmes on government policies and
activities than Network II.   A high percentage of air
time on Network II is taken up by news bulletins in four
languages - English, Chinese, Bahasa Malaysia and Indian;
whereas all the news bulletins in Network I are in the
national language.

Information and Education takes up the biggest portion
of television content - 53.4 per cent in Network I and
48.2 per cent in Network II, as shown in the programme
breakdown in table 4.1.

Many programmes are imported and are regularly among
the favourite 'top ten' - among which are syndicated films
such as 'Mannix', 'Kojak', 'Ironside', 'Mystery Movie' etc.
However, it is the government's policy to achieve a 60 per

cent target for locally produced programmes. By 1973, more than 50 per cent of programmes were local. In table 4.2 are Television Malaysia's total weekly output in terms of local content, foreign content and advertising.

TABLE 4.1   Television Malaysia, programme breakdown

Network	News	Drama	Information and education	Enter-tainment
I	13.3%	8.7%	53.4%	24.6%
II	46.0%	2.5%	48.2%	3.3%

Source: 'The Print and Broadcasting Media in Malaysia', March 1974 by South-East Asia Press Centre, Kuala Lumpur, Malaysia.

TABLE 4.2   Breakdown of television Malaysia's total weekly output

Network	Local content	Foreign content	Advertising
I	52.8%	44.7%	2.5%
II	56.8%	39.7%	3.5%

Source: 'Print and Broadcasting in Malaysia', March 1974.

Tables 4.3a and b show the breakdown of programmes for the two Television Malaysia channels for the week from 21.4.75

About half of the local programmes are on current affairs, development support and motivational. The foreign programmes mainly fall within the following four classifications: children, crime and violence or thriller, entertainment, and drama. In addition, there are also some imported foreign documentaries such as 'Science Report', 'Sport Lexicon', 'Survival', etc.

Radio Malaysia

There are at present 104 transmitting stations throughout Peninsular Malaysia. Clear reception is available in and around more densely populated areas. The physical radius

TABLE 4.3a   Breakdown of programmes on Network I for the week from 21.4.75

Programme	Bahasa Malaysia	English	Chinese	Tamil	Total	Percentage
News	5:00'00"				5:00'00"	8%
TV Malaysia Production (OR/OB)						
Local Production (film)	17:43'43"		36'59"		18:20'42"	30%
Dubbed film	2:21'45"				2:21'45"	4%
Foreign Production		29:58'54"			29:58'54"	50%
Advertising films	1:56'56"				1:56'56"	3%
Announcements	2:41'39"				2:41'39"	5%
Total	29:44'03"	29:58'54"	36'59"		60:19'56"	100%

Local Production	38%
Foreign Production	62%
Total	100%

TABLE 4.3b Breakdown of programmes on Network II for the week from 21.4.75

Programme	Bahasa Malaysia	English	Chinese	Tamil	Total	Percentage
News	7:54'13"				7:54'13"	16%
TV Malaysia Production (OR/OB)						
Local Production (film)	3:30'29"		4:34'07"	3:49'33"	11:54'09"	32%
Dubbed film						
Foreign Production		14:08'58"			14:08'58"	39%
Advertising films	21'30"	7'10"	58'50"	1'30"	1:29'00"	5%
Announcements	1:56'02"				1:56'02"	8%
Total	13:42'14"	14:16'08"	5:32'57"	3:51'03"	37:22'22"	100%

Local Production	47%
Foreign Production	53%
Total	100%

and power of each station can be found in the Appendix.
There are plans for ten more transmitters to reach the
less populated areas.

There are six regional radio stations - Penang, Ipoh,
Malacca, Kuala Trengganu, Johore Bharu, Kota Bharu - which
relay programmes from Kuala Lumpur as well as transmit
their own programmes for regional broadcast.

To reach the 60,000 Orang Asli or Aboriginese, a
special Siaran Orang Asli (Aboriginese Broadcast) was
started in 1959. Some 19 dialects are spoken by these
aboriginese but the Aboriginese Broadcast uses the Semiar
and Temiar dialects only as they form the majority groups.

Radio produces almost all of its own programmes except
for a tiny percentage of mainly scientific programmes.
The 1974 RTM Handbook gave the programmes breakdown as
shown in table 4.4

TABLE 4.4   Total weekly air time

Network	News	Information & Education	Drama	Entertainment	School Broadcast
National	7 %	23.7%	2.9%	56.9%	9.5%
Blue	10.8%	14.8%	0.8%	60.6%	13 %
Green	17.5%	18.7%	7.6%	50.3%	5.9%
Red	10.9%	17.3%	3.6%	61.7%	6.5%

The total weekly air time for each network in hours is as
follows:
National   - 168 hours
Blue   - 100 hours
Green   - 100 hours 55 mins
Red   -   92 hours 30 mins

The overseas service or Suara Malaysia (Voice of
Malaysia) broadcasts in six languages. Total weekly air
time is as follows:
Indonesian   -   56 hours
Mandarin   -   14 hours
English   -   7 hours
Thai   -   7 hours
Arabic   -   7 hours
Filipino (Tagalog, Tausug,
          Maguindaon) -   14 hours

Capital City Broadcast is on air (from 6.30 a.m. to
9.00 a.m. and 4.00 p.m. to 7.00 p.m.) for 5½ hours daily,
broadcasting brief news and weather reports, traffic situations, flight schedules, public announcements, etc. and
general musical entertainment. The FM stereo service is
on air from 9.00 a.m. to noon and 9.00 p.m. to midnight
daily. At present all the programmes are musical, with a
few minutes of local news.

Aboriginal Broadcast is on air from 2.00 p.m. to
4.00 p.m. daily. The programmes include two daily news
items of 5 minutes each. Most of the programmes are
intended to persuade the aboriginese to settle in govern-
ment-established settlements and to knit them closer to
the mainstream of Malaysia to render them less vulnerable
to communist propaganda.

3   LAWS AND REGULATIONS

On legal matters, the Department of Broadcasting uses the
Attorney-General's office but the Department has plans for
its own legal advisor, particularly for dealings with the
private sector.

Some professional staff feel they are hampered in the
scope of their work by the laws and by the fact that the
Department is a government department. This, to a certain
extent, also limits creativity. The general view among
senior Department officers is that creativity should be
confined within government policies like the New Economic
Policy, the Rukunegara, etc. There is also the practice
of self-censorship beyond the requirements of the laws and
this could be the result of senior officers, and at times,
the Deputy-Minister, viewing important programmes before
transmission.

But restrictions of this nature are generally felt
necessary in Malaysia, given the multi-racial society and
the present phase of development.

4   RELATIONSHIPS WITH OTHER NATIONAL ORGANISATIONS

Government Ministries and their affiliates may use RTM
services free. The Department of Broadcasting, being an
organ of the government, produces programmes on developmental, political and social issues, reflecting the
current policies of the government, on its own accord.

For example, if the government is encouraging people to grow their own basic food necessities, RTM will also gear its programmes to this theme. Sometimes such programmes are planned and co-ordinated with other Governmental Ministries and related organisations but only on the latter's request, and to an extent, depending on the nature of the request. Completed programmes are usually reviewed by the Deputy Minister of Information before being broadcast.

Development

The Development and Agriculture service is responsible for all development programmes over RTM. The service works closely with government development bodies and is one of the most active in the Department. Programmes range from youth and career guidance, to information for farmers. Most programmes are produced independently by the service. But the service does work with external bodies when necessary and special air time may be allocated to the development agency involved.

Education

Public Affairs Service programmes include forums, commentaries, magazines and adult education programmes. The Service also tries to bring the knowledge of law to the public through its programme 'The Law and Us'.

In the main, however, educational programmes are undertaken by Educational Television under the Ministry of Education. As well as its air time for schools, ETV has half an hour of RTM air time to cover developments in education.

Social/welfare

One of the features of the organisational structure of RTM is that the various Heads of Services are relatively free to use their discretion on producing programmes. As such, though there is no service in direct charge of social/ welfare programmes, there is a fair amount of such programming produced, especially by the Public Affairs Service and the Development and Agriculture Service.

Information

All the Services are engaged in informational activities
one way or another. Even the Entertainment and Drama
Services are engaged in this by incorporating information
on the New Economic Policy, the Green Book Plan, etc. in
their programmes. Similarly, many programmes of the
Public Affairs Service and the Development and Agriculture
Service are concerned with disseminating information about
government policies and development programmes. If there
is a nation-wide information campaign, RTM is naturally
directly involved, both in planning and implementation.

Religion

The Religious Service works in close relationship with the
Majlis Kebangsaan Kebajikan Islam, the national Islamic
council.

Programmes produced by this Service present the teach-
ings of Islam from three angles:
(a)   religious belief;
(b)   religious duties and social responsibility;
(c)   ethics and morality.

Politics

As a government agency, the Department of Broadcasting is
obliged to provide political coverage for the government.
The Public Affairs Service and the Development and
Agriculture Service provide most of the air time for this.

During national elections, the Department of Broadcasting will provide coverage under the News Division and
under the Public Affairs Service.

Television Malaysia does not provide political air time
to any political parties directly. The amount of air time
given to political broadcasting by RTM is not available.

5   PUBLIC RELATIONS AND CO-ORDINATING ACTIVITIES

Within the Department of Broadcasting, there is a General
Services Section which undertakes the public relations
activities of the Department. This section handles press
publicity, prepares slogans and announcements for

broadcast over radio and television, and is responsible
for all RTM publications. It liaises with overseas
broadcasting organisations, answers queries and verifies
reception reports of overseas listeners. In addition, it
organises visits for the thousands of visitors to Angkasapuri every year and looks after the distribution of
tickets for all radio and television shows.

Within the Ministry of Information, there is a section
in the Research and Evaluation Division which handles
public relations work for the Ministry. Among some of the
functions of this section are:

(a)   to advise other Ministries and governmental agencies
      on media and communication problems;
(b)   to co-ordinate with other Ministries in the launching
      of national campaigns;
(c)   to co-ordinate with statutory and other bodies/
      agencies like the Federal Land Development Agency
      (FELDA), the Rubber Research Institute (RRI), the
      universities, etc., when the need arises;
(d)   to help and advise in planning campaigns by other
      Ministries for implementation by the Ministry of
      Information;
(e)   to undertake normal publicity activities, such as
      press liaison, etc.;
(f)   to meet and brief visitors and organised groups to
      RTM;
(g)   to co-ordinate attachment programmes of officers to
      the Ministry.

The Section is also involved in procuring materials
needed for campaigns and, at times, in writing specialised releases and speeches for senior officials etc.

The Ministry, through this section, also participates
in joint activities with external bodies. The Ministry
has advised and helped plan communication strategy for
bodies like the Malaysian Handicraft Board, Bank Simpanan
Nasional (The National Saving Bank), and even commercial
bodies like the Malaysian Development Bank.

Officers of this section, and also from the Public
Affairs Service, normally represent the Ministry and the
Department of Broadcasting in the committees of other
government departments and statutory bodies so as to
assist them in carrying out their programmes effectively.
They are also voting members of many such committees
examples of which are the National Family Planning Board
and the Task Force on Price Control. The Ministry also

maintains close relationships with the press and there is
a certain amount of co-ordination, especially on an informal and unofficial basis.

These public relation activities are free.

In addition to the co-ordinating activities undertaken
by the two sections mentioned, various services may undertake their own co-ordinating activities. For example,
the Aboriginese Broadcast service has a co-ordinating
committee called the Jawatan Penyelaras Siaran Orang Asli
composed of members of Radio Malaysia and the Aboriginese
Department, Ministry of Rural Development, while Radio
Ibukota co-ordinates with the Traffic Department through a
special appointed officer of the Traffic Department.

RTM is a member of ABU, AMIC and Commonwelath Broadcasting Union. It is an associated member of European
Broadcasting Union. Through its 'Voice of Malaysia'
service, it exchanges programmes with the US Information
Service and sends programmes to local stations in Indonesia for repeat broadcasts.

6   FINANCE

As is the normal procedure of any government department,
RTM draws up a proposed budget annually for the coming
year's expenditure. The various divisions of the Department of Broadcasting each send an estimate of their
expenditure to their respective controllers who review it
before sending it to the Cabinet for approval, via the
Ministry of Information.

TABLE 4.5 Estimates of expected expenditure for 1976

Operating expenditure of RTM	M$79,789,800
Development expenditure of RTM	M$15,241,270
Total:	M$95,031,071

The above estimated sum has been submitted to the
government Treasury for consideration and incorporation
into the Third Malaysia Plan (1976-1980), details of which
have yet to be released.

Under the Second Malaysia Plan (1971-5) M$45.73 million

(0.63 per cent of the total sum of the M$7,250 million allocated for public development expenditure) was allocated to the Department of Broadcasting for its development expenditure in Peninsular Malaysia. This was raised to M$57.88 million during the mid-term revision of the Plan, and represented 0.62 per cent of the revised public development expenditure of M$9,350 million. Development expenditure of the Department of Broadcasting in Peninsular Malaysia for the period 1971-3 was estimated to be M$33.27 million with M$24.61 million still to be spent by the end of the Plan period. The breakdown of operating and development expenditures of the Department of Broadcasting is not available.

The Department received no other income, all revenue from the sale of air time and licences being channelled back directly to the government Treasury. The advertising and licence revenue usually covers about 1/3 of all expenditure of RTM. In 1974 radio and television licences brought in about M$17.01 million, and advertising raised more than M$16 million. The sale of transcription records and video tapes was estimated to have brought in a further M$4,000.

7   BROADCASTING OUTPUT

News

RTM now has a 24-hour news service. All information gathered is edited by the various bulletin editors supervised by the Senior News Editor in RTM. As stated previously, local news is given preference and within local news, priority is given to items that promote government images and policies. For example, the government is at the moment encouraging people to plant vegetables and fruit in their home surroundings to beat inflationary prices. Hence any incident that highlights such government emphasis will be given very high priority. Generally, preference for local news is given to:
(a)   reports that have important impact on Malaysians; and
(b)   reports that support the principles of Rukunegara, the New Economic Policy, and the second Malaysia plan.

Within a news bulletin, the percentage of foreign news can range from nil to 50 per cent but is usually not more than 40 per cent.

Television Malaysia broadcasts seven bulletins daily, with the breakdown of television news as shown in tables 4.6a and b.

TABLE 4.6a   Breakdown of television news (Network I)

Language	Time of telecast	Duration
Bahasa Malaysia	6.00 p.m.	10 minutes
Bahasa Malaysia	9.00 p.m.	20 minutes
Bahasa Malaysia	11.00 p.m.	10 minutes

TABLE 4.6b   Breakdown of television news (Network II)

Language	Time of telecast	Duration
Tamil	7.00 p.m.	15 minutes
Mandarin	8.00 p.m.	15 minutes
Bahasa Malaysia	9.00 p.m.	20 minutes
English	10.00 p.m.	15 minutes

Radio Malaysia broadcasts 46 national news bulletins a day, one of which, on the national network, is a major news bulletin lasting 30 minutes. This is excluding the regional news broadcast daily over Kuala Lumpur, Kota Kinabalu, Kuching, Pulau Pinang, Johore Bharu, and Kuala Trengganu, and the news services for Aborigines and over-seas countries.

The breakdown of radio news is as shown in tables 4.7a and b.

Information and education

Most educational television programmes are produced by RTM in the form of talks, features, documentaries, forums and interviews. This Information and Education category comprises the major portion of the overall programmes' content in both networks - 53.4 per cent in Network I and 48.2 per cent in Network II. Programmes broadcast include 'Forun', 'Komentar' (Commentaries), 'Scope' etc. To supplement the locally-produced programmes, documentaries such as 'Science Report', 'Survival', etc. are imported.

TABLE 4.7a   Breakdown of radio news (domestic networks)[*]

Language	No. of bulletins	Duration
Bahasa Malaysia	19	249 minutes
English	7	65 minutes
Chinese	13	120 minutes
Tamil	7	60 minutes

TABLE 4.7b   Breakdown of radio news (overseas service)[*]

Language	No. of bulletins	Duration
Indonesian	7	65 minutes
English	2	20 minutes
Mandarin	2	20 minutes
Thai	1	10 minutes
Arabic	1	10 minutes
Bahasa Malaysia	1	5 minutes
Tagalog	1	10 minutes

*Source: RTM Handbook, 1974.

The educational radio programmes are all locally pro-
duced by RTM - such as 'Window on the World', 'Sikap
Baru' (New Attitudes), 'The Law and Us', and 'Hidup
Bersama' (Living Together). Next to Entertainment,
Information and Education occupies the largest percentage
of content on the four radio networks.

Editorial control of such programmes is exercised on a
day-to-day basis during weekly meetings with the Deputy
Minister of Information and other division heads. Problems are dealt with as they arise.

Taboo subject matters and topics are those that contravene the principles of Rukunegara or touch on matters considered 'seditious'. All programmes are covered in this
way.

Political broadcasting

Political broadcasting during national elections over
Television Malaysia is confined to news coverage and
special informational programmes.

The breakdown on political broadcasting air time is not
available.

8 PRODUCTION

The Film Procurement Section in RTM is responsible for
renting documentaries and feature films. Among the main
suppliers are Twentieth Century-Fox, MGM, Columbia Pic-
tures, United Artists, the British Broadcasting Corporation and Deutsche Welle. The rates for such films from
commercial suppliers are usually US$110 per one-hour pro-
gramme and US$55 per ½ hour programme, paid from RTM
funds.

After the films have been checked and reviewed by
RTM's Programme Committee, a contract is signed whereby
the number of episodes/series, time wanted etc., is
stated. In 1974, 145 such contracts were signed and
these included cartoons, soccer, features, etc., and each
contract may have as many as twenty-six episodes. Local
productions are self-produced.

9 ORGANISATION OF TECHNICAL SERVICES

Organisational structure

Technical services for the production and transmission of
radio and television programmes for the Department of
Broadcasting is provided for by the Engineering Division.

The structure of the Division is as shown in figure 2.

Co-ordination

All technical facilities for the production and transmission of radio and television programmes are provided by
the Operations and Maintenance Section. The section
liaises with the Programme Division and provides the
necessary technical facilities. A listening room is
maintained to check on the quality of all transmissions
and productions.

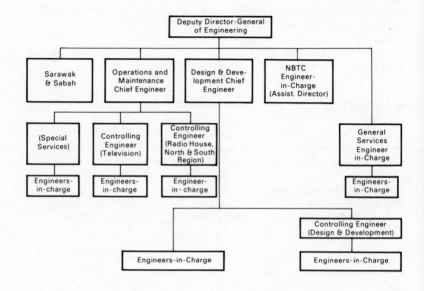

FIGURE 2   Structure of the Engineering Division

Programme staff, like producers, are required to list
their technical requirements in advance. The Engineer-
in-Charge of the particular section will then try to meet
the requirements.

Finished recordings for broadcast are sent to the Tape
Room with specifications written on them (title, date of
broadcast, etc). The tapes are then arranged according to
programme schedules and are sent to transmission studios
on the day and time required. The transmission studios
broadcast the programmes to the listeners through the
Master Control Room (MCR). In the case of television
video-tapes, the recorded tape is kept in the Tape Room
and will be sent to the library the following day. From
there, the script assistant in charge of a particular programme will book for transmission via the library, the
Tape Room, the continuity suite and the MCR.

Television programmes are channelled to the Telecommunications Switching Centre in Bukit Nanas, Kuala
Lumpur by underground coaxial cables for distribution to

the north, south and east of Peninsular Malaysia for transmission by a permanent network of transmitters linked by
microwave. Radio programmes are channelled to the other
station via Telecoms or via cables to the Kajang transmitters.

   The following are the sections which have an Engineer-
in-Charge:
1. Special Services
      (a)   Store and Equipment (Studio) section
      (b)   ETV section
      (c)   Filem Negara section
      (d)   Plant Services section
      (e)   Film Divison, Television section

2. Television
      (a)   Studio section
      (b)   Outdoor Broadcast section
      (c)   Master Control Room
      (d)   Video-tape recorder
      (e)   Telecine

3. Radio House, North and East Regions
      (a)   Radio House
      (b)   Ipoh
      (c)   Penang
      (d)   Kuala Trengganu
      (e)   Kota Bharu

4. Kajang and South Region
      (a)   Kajang - National Network
      (b)   Kajang - Overseas
      (c)   Kajang - Transmitting aerial and store
      (d)   Malacca
      (e)   Johore Bharu

5. Design and Development
      There are 7 engineers-in-charge, all are in charge
      of projects.

6. National Broadcasting Training Centre
      (a)   Studio
      (b)   Engineering Training
      (c)   Radio Training
      (d)   Television Training
      There is also an engineer-in-charge who heads the
      above 4 sections. He is also an assistant director
      of NBTC.

7. General Services
   There is only one engineer-in-charge in this section.

The above engineers-in-charge liaise directly with the
production staff to fulfill their technical requirements.

Technical facilities

Television Malaysia   Television Malaysia uses the 625-
line monochrome television system. Television House at
Angkasapuri, Kuala Lumpur is a three-storey building which
accommodates all the production, technical, design and
staging, and film facilities. It has 4 studios, the
largest of which is 80 foot by 60 foot, 3 continuity
suites, 4 16mm telecine chains, 2 35mm telecine chains,
5 16mm magnetic film reproducers, 8 video tape recorders,
10 camera chains, 3 studio transmitter links, 2 subtitling
units, 1 caption scanner, 1 telecorder with a 16mm magnetic film recorder/reproducer, together with all other
associated equipment. The outdoor broadcasting facilities
consist of 1 three-camera mobile unit and 1 four-camera
mobile unit. A third mobile cruiser unit is equipped with
a two-camera chain and a video tape-recorder.

The electronic system is fully transistorised and
colour compatible. It is based on the centralised equipment and systems design concept. It provides for an economic and efficient future expansion through the use of a
delegate switching system.

The studios have ten $4\frac{1}{2}$ transistorised image orthicon
cameras. In all the studios, light dimming equipment,
visual prompter and rear screen projection operation
facilities are provided. Two special effects generators
and two subtitling units may be delegated to any one of
the studios and continuity suites from the master control
room.

Each of the announcement booths, which are part of the
3 continuity suites, are equipped with a vidicon camera.
The camera control units of all the television cameras are
located in the camera control unit room which is part of
the centralised system.

Radio Malaysia   All equipment in Radio House is fully
transistorised and the facility for musical recording in
stereophonic sound is available. There are 6 drama
studios equipped with facilities for special purposes such

as sound effects, etc. Each of these suites has a console
with twelve channels, three gramophones and two reel-to-
reel tape recorders. There is a music studio with similar
equipment as that in the drama studios but without special
sound effects facilities, and a talks studio with one console, two reel-to-reel recorders, and three turntables.

There are 8 transmission studios, each equipped with
two console units, two playback machines, three casette
recorders and three turntables. There are also 8 editing
rooms.

A separate room with equipment for special recording is
also available. This is the Recording Room which has
three sets of duplication machines, three to ten low
speed recorders, a commercial disc cutter, eight logging
machines and a machine for checking and reclaiming old
tapes.

There are in addition 2 halls, one with 250 seats and
the other 1,000. Both possess special lighting and
stereophonic facilities.

10 ADMINISTRATION

The Department of Broadcasting is headed by the Director-
General of Broadcasting, assisted by the Deputy Director-
General of Engineering and the Deputy Director-General of
Programming. In matters concerning general administra-
tion, he is assisted by the Head of Administration,
Services and Establishment and the Head of Finance. The
Directors of the various regional stations are directly
responsible to him.

Engineering and technical services are under the
Deputy Director-General in charge of engineering,
assisted by two chief engineers. Under them are the
various Chief Engineers and Engineers-in-Charge of
various divisions and services.

The various services of RTM, such as drama, current
affairs, etc., are under the charge of Heads who liaise
with the Controllers of Radio and Television. The Controllers, together with the Head of News Division, are
responsible to the Deputy Director-General in charge of
programming.

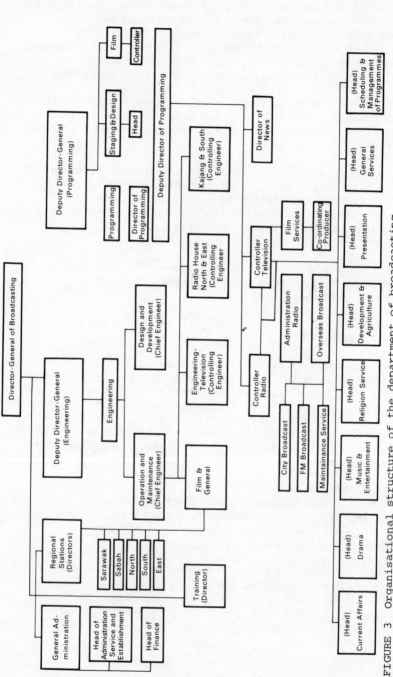

FIGURE 3 Organisational structure of the department of broadcasting

Grade and salary structures

The services of the monthly rated staff in the Department
of Broadcasting are divided into four divisions/groups;
and their salary scales are according to the Suffian
Salary Commission, which applies to the Government Services as a whole.

The grade and salary structures of RTM staff are divided into the four following groups:
(a) Managerial and professional group
This category includes administrative officers with high
educational qualifications (usually a tertiary degree),
professional officers, and others especially qualified
by training and experience for senior posts. The minimum
level of salary scale for the managerial and professional
personnel is about M$1,200 per month with the maximum
salary in this scale not fixed.
(b) Executive and sub-professional group
The minimum qualification for this level is the Higher
School Certificate (HSC) or a Diploma. The basic salary
scale of this division is between M$700 to M$1,200 per
month.
(c) Clerical and technical group
Those belonging to this category require a good secondary
school education and the basic qualification of a Malaysian Certificate of Education (MCE). The basic salary
scale of the clerical and technical group is between
M$250 - M$750 per month.
(d) Industrial and manual group (IMG)
This includes those whose occupations range from the
unskilled to the highly skilled and can be broadly
divided into three groups - general labour, semi-skilled
labour, and the artisan group. The basic salary for the
IMG is less than M$250 per month.

Although the basic salary structures remain, the salary
scheme as a whole may be revised from time to time as the
need arises.

The general pattern of the salary scales which are at
present in force appears to be of two types. In the various Division/Groups, the pattern generally is a long time
scale of about 15 to 20 steps, whereas with the IMG
grades, a shorter time scale of not more than three or
four steps is more common. One of the defects of the long
time scale is that it is possible for an employee to
receive increments annually up to the maximum of the time-
scale while he continues to do the same job. The

contention is that this would be contrary to the principle
of the rate for the job. Hence the Suffian Salary Commission has reduced these long time scales resulting in the
grant of higher initial salaries. In other cases, the
Suffian Commission has broken up the time scale into two
or more grades, again to ensure that the nature of the
duties carried out justifies the salary scale offered.

Recruitment

Candidates for posts within the purview of a Service Commission are selected by the Public Services Commission
following advertisements in the local newspapers and in
the government 'Gazette'. Posts which are to be filled by
officers in 'closed services' are advertised by departmental circulars only, while posts which are open only to
serving officers are advertised in the government
'Gazette'.

Promotion

Generally, schemes of service provide avenues of promotion
to higher grades within the same scheme. There are also
avenues of promotion for certain categories of officers
in one service to another higher service. Promotion to
higher grades within the same service sometimes depends on
the officers passing the departmental examinations/
efficiency bars/interviews prescribed by their schemes.

Unions

All governmental broadcasting services fall under the
category of 'essential services' and as such, broadcasting
personnel are not allowed to go on strike, or to take any
other form of industrial action.

Previously, RTM's staff had their own union, the
Broadcasting Union, which is now merged in a larger union,
the National Union of Employees in the Ministry of Inform-
ation. This National Union is affiliated to Cuepacs, the
Congress of Union of Employees in Public and Civil
Services.

There is also the Malayan Technical Union for technicians. The Senior Officers Association/Club, as the name
suggests, is strictly for all senior administrative

officers, senior technical engineers, etc. of all government departments, including RTM.

In terms of the relationship between RTM's administration and the staff union and professional union, there are
no regular and rigid procedures such as monthly meetings,
etc. All suggestions, complaints and negotiations take
place on an irregular basis although there is a staff welfare officer in the administration who looks after the
problems of staff members. This service is, however, confined to the staff at Headquarters in Kuala Lumpur.

It is generally acknowledged by RTM's staff that there
is a communication gap between the administration, composed of Malay Civil Service (MCS) officers, and the professional and technical staff, a number of whom are on
contract or are part-timers. To fill this gap a special
officer seconded from the professional staff, i.e. the
Department of Broadcasting, is included in the administration whose main function is to advice the MCS officers on
any problems in their dealings with the professional
staff.

11   TRAINING BY THE ORGANISATION

The National Broadcasting Training Centre (NBTC) provides
the necessary training to personnel in the Department of
Broadcasting whenever the need arises.

Established in late 1970, NBTC became operational from
December 1971, at its temporary premises at Dewan Tunku
Abdul Rahman, Jalan Ampang. The Centre is now in the process of developing a permanent broadcasting training
centre at Angkasapuri which will have 2 studios (including
1 for colour training), 3 radio studios, 9 classrooms,
film, design, news and laboratory training areas and other
ancillary and technical facilities for training. A hostel
block that can accommodate 80 trainees and a dining block
that could cater for 150 persons at any one time will also
be part of the new training complex. This scheme will
cost about M$11 million.

The Centre provides full-time, in-service and part-time
training in the fields of production and programming,
engineering, technical operations, film, news, stage,
design and graphics, research and utilisation, and broadcast administration.

   The courses given are carried out in four stages;
induction, basic, intermediate, and advanced training.
The courses range from one or two days each to twelve or
more weeks. Each course will have a maximum of 15 to 20
trainees with an intake of 100-150 full-time students.
Part-time students may reach a total of 300-500 students
annually.

   In addition NBTC also provides training staff and other
facilities for the ASIAN Institute of Broadcast Development under ABU and in close collaboration with UNESCO.
All members of ABU are given intermediate and advanced
training at the NBTC. The regional training activities
involve not only training courses but include seminars
and workshops.

   The Centre also undertakes familiarisation, appreciation and orientation courses for planners, administrators and others whose work involved co-operation with
broadcasters.

   Apart from lecture notes and publication materials on
each of the subjects taught, the teaching aids include
overhead projectors, slides, film shows, video tapes and
cartridge films. For practical work, the facilities used
include practical kits, meter bridges, tools for soldering
exercises, audio-oscillators, etc.

Training facilities (hardware)

The present complex at Jalan Ampang has a radio and a
television studio. The facilities are as shown in table
4.8

   The MCR has transmission facilities, its own power supplies and video and audio amplifiers.

Radio studio

The radio studio is partitioned into the talks studio, the
drama studio and the recording and editing section. The
radio studio has the facilities shown in table 4.10.

Fees, staff and services

No fees are charged by the Centre for the training and the

TABLE 4.8   Training facilities of the NBTC

Equipment	Description
Television Studio	
3 cameras (EMI)	2 zoom 1 turret Each camera, 20 amps
20 dimmers (Strand)	Each 20 amps
1 AB switcher (EMI)	With special effects and keying facilities
1 audio control console	8 channels
10 microphones	1 boom 1 condenser 5 ribbon 3 neck (moving coil)
1 tape-recorder (Ampex)	Reel-to-reel
2 gramophones (Philips)	
Telecine	
1 Marconi Telecine Chain	Vidicon
2 film projectors	16mm
1 slide projector	35mm, 60 slides
1 Westrex magnetic recorder and reproducer	16mm
1 Ampex 1200B VTR	With Editex facilities
2 helical scanners	1 with time base corrector 1 without time base corrector
Master Control Room	
2 Marconi Sync-Pulse Generators	With change-over facilities
1 VI Module	

TABLE 4.9 Facilities available for outdoor broadcasts at NBTC

Equipment	Description
1 van	
2 cameras	Plumbicon
1 caption scanner	
1 helical scanner	
1 audio mixer	6 channel
1 video switcher	With special effects and keying facilities
Facilities for microwave links for transmission	
Microwave links for receiver for recording	

TABLE 4.10 Facilities of the radio studio at NBTC

Equipment	Description
Studio recording	
5 Ampex recorder and reproducer machines	
6 Philips Heavy Duty turntables	
2 audio mixers	1 with 6 channels 1 with 2 channels
10 microphones	3 condenser 5 ribbon 2 combination ribbon and moving coil

For Outside recording

1 tape-deck	Cassette
1 audio mixer	4 channel
2 Tanberg tape-recorders	Reel-to-reel
3 Nagra tape-recorders	Reel-to-reel
10 tape-recorders	Cassette

use of facilities by the trainees. Upon completion of the course, a trainee goes back to the organisation. Only the regional trainees are awarded with certificates after completing the training courses.

Each year the Centre will draw up a proposed budget for the whole year; and this will be submitted to the federal Treasury. The proposed budget for 1975 was estimated to be M$1.5 million.

The Centre's 20-odd training staff and the numerous supporting staff of technicians, laboratory assistants, maintenance personnel and projectionists, etc. are seconded from the Department of Broadcasting. Four UNESCO Advisors were sent to the Centre in 1974 and one in 1975.

The Training Centre is considered an essential service (like the army, telecommunications, police etc.) and although members of the staff are allowed to join the Broadcasting Union, they are not allowed to go on strike.

The Centre also provides training for members from the Police, Malaysian Airline Service, Ministry of Defence, Universiti Sains Malaysia, Mara College, Ministry of Youth and Culture, through the Ministry of Information.

12   TRAINING BY OTHER BODIES

The Universiti Sains Malaysia provides a programme in Mass Communications whereby serving officers in the Ministry may enrol to attain a tertiary degree.

The Educational Technology Unit (ETU) at the University has the basic facilities for training in broadcasting. Apart from training education students in the use of

TABLE 4.11   Summary of courses/work load for 1972, 1973, and 1974

Courses		Total no. of courses			Total courses per week/year			Total no. of trainees		
		72	73	74	72	73	74	72	73	74
Production and presentation	Production (TV)	11	6	13	25	17	27	70	35	166
	Production (Radio)	9	19	19	16	31	36	102	251	303
	Film	4	8	11	8	12	28	32	58	97
Engineering and operations	Engineering	7	4	3	45	38	33	139	107	44
	Operations (TV)	5	8	8	30	27	26	58	79	82
	Operations (Radio)			2			9			45
Extension services	Regular courses	3	5	5	12	24	25	45	72	92
	Seminar/ workshop	2	3	6	1	3	6	25	27	80
	Production of manuals									
	Production of films									
Grand Total		41	53	67	137	152	190	471	629	909

TABLE 4.12   Proposed courses for 1975

Type of course	No. of courses	Total no. of weeks
Radio production training	25	23
Television technical operation training	13	34
Television production training	12	34
Film training programme	11	33
Engineering training programme	5	56
Regional training course	8	26

audio-visual aids, the ETU also aims at providing the opportunity for communication students to do practical work in broadcasting and audio-visual media for the mass media.

The Unit was built with the aid of a World Bank loan. The initial equipment, costing M$486,935.85 was purchased through the World Bank. The building costs of about M$772,000 were paid by the Malaysian Government through the University. The Malaysian Government is also covering the operational expenditure of the Unit.

For the academic year 1974/5, 240 education students did basic courses in educational resources. 46 communication students attended courses in curriculum development under an educational psychologist.

The Unit provides in-service courses for its technicians. Together with the Ministry of Education and the Mass Communication Programme in the School of Humanities, the Unit is running a one-year certificate course in educational broadcasting to train personnel for the Educational Media Service. There are also plans to provide courses, especially in educational technology, for lecturers in Teacher Training Colleges and for practising teachers. Plans are being made to revise present educational technology and communication courses.

The Unit has a photographic service, a media library,
an equipment loan service, projection and viewing services, sound production and recording services, television
production and recording services and a graphics and
illustration service.

Hardware

Television   There is a three-camera studio with 2 sync-
pulse generators, a vision switcher that can accommodate
6 sources, 9 monitors, 1 audio console with 6 microphone
channels, and 4 high-level channels. The lighting dimmer
has a 40 unit capability.

The telecine, VTR and MCR are housed together in a
single unit. There are 2 open reel 1" VTR, 8 cartridge
1" VTR, 1 16mm film projector, 2 35mm slide projectors,
1 vidicon chain, 3 television tuners and a test signal
generator.

Radio   There is one studio with 5 electric condenser
microphones, 2 turntables, 2 reel-to-reel tape-recorders
and an audio console with 6 microphone channels and 4
high-level channels.

There are no transmission facilities. In-campus relay
of radio programmes produced by students is done through
cables connected to speakers placed at strategic points.

The Institute of Technology, Mara, provides another
possible source of professional communicators through its
School of Mass Communication. Though the three-year
programme lays emphasis on journalism, advertising and
public relations, writing for broadcast is also taught.

The entry requirement for the course at the Institute
is the Higher School Certificate, with principal-level
passes in English and Bahasa Malaysia, one subsidiary
level pass and a pass in the General paper.

Applicants with the General Certificate of Education at
the Advanced level, with 'A' (Advanced) level passes in
English and one other subject, 'O' (Ordinary) level pass
and a pass in the General Paper, are also accepted.

Applicants with at least four years experience in the
mass media and who have obtained a total of five credits
in the Malaysian Certificate of Education examination may
also be considered.

Students of the programme have access to RTM facilities for their broadcast practical training.

13   RESEARCH

Research on broadcasting is part of the Ministry of Information's activities for the RTM which, at present, does not have a research division of its own.

Since this section is newly established under the Research and Planning Division of the Ministry, most of the research done so far has been carried out by outside/commercial research agencies. Studies on television ratings and radio ratings, for example, have been commissioned from a commercial research agency. The priority at the time this report was written, was on collecting information for radio and television producers as to what kind of programmes to produce and in what format.

The structure of this small research section is being planned. At the time of writing, there were four research assistants working under the Head of this research section who also have to carry out research projects for the Department of Information Services. Among the studies conducted for the Department of Information Services are the Village Survey (with a national sample) on Media Information Exposure and the effects of the Mobile Information Units.

Funds for all these research projects come directly from the Ministry of Information, and not from the budget of the Department of Broadcasting (RTM) or the Department of Information Services. Therefore, due to the limitation of staff and funds, the selection of any research project is based mainly on the urgency and relevance of present needs.

It is hoped that in the near future communication research activities will be expanded with the co-operation of other government research agencies and universities. Collation of research results on communication activities done by the various organisations is required. Hence the need to have a clearing house of communication research findings which will serve as a communication data bank. This kind of data bank could avoid duplication of communication research activities and stimulate a better co-ordination among communication agencies.

Chapter 5

ORGANISATION AND PROCESSES OF THE RADIO ROYAL AUSTRALIAN AIR FORCE, Butterworth

The only foreign-owned radio station allowed in Malaysia, Radio RAAF's main aim is to entertain RAAF personnel and their families although information and education is also provided.

The station covers a ten miles radius from the RAAF base which is situated in Butterworth, Penang. Radio RAAF begins broadcasting from 6.00 a.m. till 11.30 p.m. on Sundays through Thursday and from 6.00 a.m. till 1.00 p.m. on Fridays and Saturdays. Thus the total weekly air time is $125\frac{1}{2}$ hours.

TABLE 5.1 Breakdown for various categories of programmes

Programmes	Time
Musical	79 hours
News	$27\frac{1}{2}$ hours
Sports	$5\frac{1}{2}$ hours
Comedy	1 hour
Children's	3 hours
Talks and serials	9 hours

There is no quota on either the kind or amount of imported materials nor on the percentage of news and entertainment broadcast. Most of the programmes are relayed from the ABC (Australian Broadcasting Corporation).

Radio RAAF observes the conditions laid down by a charter issued by the Malaysian Government. Some of the conditions stipulated are:

(a) to send a monthly report on the kinds of programmes broadcast to the Ministry of Information;

(b) decrease transmitter power from 1 KW to 500 watts, limiting the physical radius to approximately ten miles;

(c) no advertising;

(d) observe all international conditions;

(e) must not broadcast any material that offends morals, religion or any institution in Malaysia;

(f) Ministry of Information should be allowed to use Radio RAAF whenever the need arises;

(g) no political broadcasts.

There is no formal relationship between Radio RAAF and other national organisation/voluntary or specific interest groups, although the station may accept requests for any public service announcements.

Dealings with the Malaysian Government are through the Australian Embassy and the Australian Ministry of Defence. On the international level, Radio RAAF has membership with only the Australian Broadcasting Corporation (ABC).

Radio RAAF is financed from the RAAF Welfare Fund which is based in Australia, with a sub-committee in Butterworth. As the station gets its relay programmes from ABC free of charge and makes no payment to its volunteer personnel, most of its expenditure is on equipment - for example the purchase of records, repair facilities, power usage, etc. Radio RAAF has to account for its expenditure to the Welfare Fund annually and the Fund's committee then decides on the allocation of income. (The figures of expenditure are not revealed.)

Radio RAAF is required to broadcast daily $2\frac{1}{2}$ hours of news from Radio Television Malaysia. The station may also broadcast other programmes from RTM besides the news programmes. It also gets its news relayed from ABC and in this case, editorial control is mainly a matter of self-censorship by the station's personnel using the charter as a guideline.

Information-educational programmes are mostly in the form of talks and serials, all of which are relayed from the ABC.

Except for the musical programme (providing request songs in the station's recording studio), Radio RAAF does not produce any programme. A technical officer is in charge of all technical facilities, and he liaises with other personnel for the production of the daily musical programme and facilitates the relay process from Australia.

In 1975, Radio RAAF had the following facilities: 3 studios (amplified), 9 turntables, 2 cassette decks, 2 transmitters (one of which is for emergency purposes), 2 receivers to relay programmes. All equipment belongs to the RAAF Welfare Fund.

Administratively, Radio RAAF is divided into four:
(a)   administration of the station under the charge of the station manager;
(b)   production, under the charge of another station manager;
(c)   property, which is the responsibility of a property officer;
(d)   technical facilities, controlled by a technical officer.

All the above four officers are responsible to the Officer-in-Charge of the station. The managing personnel are appointed but they reserve the right to refuse. They are not required to possess previous broadcasting experience but preference is given to those who have. Like all other members of the staff, they work on a volunteer basis.

About 120 persons work in Radio RAAF, all on a part-time basis. They are either RAAF personnel or members of their families.

ORGANISATION AND PROCESSES OF THE EDUCATIONAL MEDIA SERVICE

1 GENERAL OBJECTIVES AND FUNCTIONS

The Educational Media Service (EMS) Division of the
Ministry of Education was established in early 1972. The
main reason for the formation of the Division was to co-
ordinate the work done by Educational Television, Schools
Radio and the Audio-Visual Aids (AVA) services.

Among some of the objectives of the EMS Division are:
(a) to supplement the educational programme in schools,
     especially in the rural schools;
(b) to aid in the teaching of science and mathematics;
(c) to aid in the teaching of technical and vocational
     subjects;
(d) to encourage awareness of civics;
(e) to enhance the standard of Bahasa Malaysia and
     English;
(f) to enhance and widen the teaching of the humanities
     and other subjects like art and handicrafts, physi-
     cal education and music;
(g) to disseminate information regarding educational
     matters to parents and to inform teachers regarding
     changes and activities in the field of education
     through the programme 'Alam Pendidikan'.

The main functions of the three sections of the EMS
Division are:
(a) to plan and produce broadcasts for schools through
     ETV;
(b) to plan and produce broadcasts for schools through
     Schools Radio;
(c) to plan, produce and distribute AVA materials to
     schools and other institutions;

(d)   to run and co-ordinate a film library service, the
      loan of educational films and AVA materials to
      schools.

The objective of ETV and Schools Radio is to aid the
Ministry of Education in its endeavour to implement the
objectives of the Malaysian Educational System.

2   COVERAGE

There are about 4,400 schools in Peninsular Malaysia but
only about 1,200 schools have radio sets. In the case
of ETV, the government is easing the problem by distribut-
ing 5,500 television sets and 2,500 generators to
schools. Even then, it is estimated that out of the
63,033 teachers in Peninsular Malaysia, only about 5,000
use ETV programmes in their teaching.

Since schools in Malaysia have two sessions daily, one
in the morning and one in the afternoon, EMS broadcasts
each programme twice daily. Programmes are repeated over
a two-week period to ensure the widest coverage possible.

All programmes for schools are structured after the
school syllabus. The aim is to complement and supplement
what is being taught in schools. Representatives from
the Ministry of Information and subject-matter advisors
ensure that programmes produced conform to the school
syllabus determined by the Ministry of Education.

Programmes intended for general audiences and teachers
are developed by EMS independently but they still have to
conform to national educational objectives.

3   LAWS AND REGULATIONS

There are certain policies regarding racial composition
and racial stereotypes which the EMS is required to note
in its productions. Apart from this, producers are completely free within the context of their subject area.

4   RELATIONSHIPS WITH OTHER NATIONAL
ORGANISATIONS/PUBLIC RELATIONS ACTIVITIES

The Educational Media Service works closely with other
divisions of the Ministry of Education and the Department

of Broadcasting to implement the national educational
objectives. Representatives are invited from the
Curriculum Development Centre and other divisions to help
plan the programmes undertaken by EMS.

There is also a close relationship with the Centre of
Educational Development Overseas (CEDO) in London,
especially in training and in the production of programmes.
Training is also provided by Universiti Sains Malaysia
and the National Broadcasting Training Centre.

EMS does not have any formal relationship with voluntary or specific interest groups but will request their
assistance if their participation is required in the production of programmes. An example is the production of
the radio programme 'Sejarah Tanah Air' or Malaysian
History which is produced with the co-operation of the
History Association of Malaysia.

Public relations activities are handled by the publications unit which prints pamphlets and other informational materials on EMS for public consumption. This is
in addition to its main function of providing necessary
materials such as notes, time-tables, etc. required by
teachers.

5 FINANCE

The development expenditure of ETV under the Second Malaysia Plan was originally M$10 million. But this was
increased to M$11,397,000 during the mid-term review of
the Plan. About M$4,940,000 of that sum is a loan from
the World Bank. The balance of M$6,457,000 is from the
Malaysian Government. Schools Radio operates on an
annual budget of M$800,000 from the Ministry of Education.

The operating expenditure of ETV for 1972, the year it
began its service, was M$698,000. In 1973, with the
increase in the number of programmes and personnel, the
sum was M$1,309,886 and in 1974 the sum was M$1.4 million.
This sum includes the M$900,000 EMS has to pay annually
for salaries, M$30,000 - 40,000 for expenditure on facili-
ties and M$900,000 paid to the Ministry of Information for
the use of RTM facilities. This M$900,000 to the Ministry
of Information includes M$190,000 paid to the Telecommuni-
cations Department for the use of transmission facilities.

A large percentage of the M$11,397,000 allocated under

the Second Malaysia Plan is expected to be used for the
purchase of television sets and generators, and the building of a new television studio.

6   BROADCAST OUTPUT

Educational television

Educational Television will be producing 30 series in
1975. All the programmes are local productions except for
occasional film inserts. ETV programmes are broadcast
over Network I on Mondays and Tuesdays and over Network II
on Wednesdays and Thursdays. There are no broadcasts on
Fridays, Saturdays and Sundays because some states have
their weekend holidays on Fridays and Saturdays, while
others have theirs on Saturdays and Sundays. The average
weekly air time for ETV broadcasts to primary schools is 8
hours, while the average weekly air time for broadcasts to
secondary schools is 14 hours 20 minutes. They normally
start at 7.40 a.m. and end at 5.20 p.m.

    Given in tables 6.1a and b are the names of the series
that were broadcast in 1975, the number of programmes in
each series and the number of times each programme in the
series was broadcast.

    All programmes for primary schools last 15 minutes.
Programmes for secondary schools normally last 20 minutes.
Of the 30 series, science programmes form 33.3 per cent of
the total, mathematics programmes form 30 per cent, while
the remaining 36.7 per cent is taken up by commercial
studies, civics, information programmes to teachers and
languages.

Schools radio

Schools radio broadcasts in four languages, namely,
Bahasa Malaysia, English, Chinese (Mandarin) and Tamil.
Like ETV, Schools Radio also broadcasts only on Mondays,
Tuesdays, Wednesdays and Thursdays. The average weekly
air time is 41 hours. The breakdown is as follows:
National Network   16 hours (for National schools)
Blue Network   13 hours (for English medium
                        schools)
Green Network   6 hours (for Chinese medium
                        schools)
Red Network   6 hours (for Tamil medium schools)

TABLE 6.1a   School broadcast outputs: Primary school

Series		Level	No. of pro-grammes	No. of times each pro-gramme will be broadcast
1	Bahasa Malaysia	Standard 3	10	4
2	English language	Standard 4	9	4
3	Science	Standard 4	19	5
4	Mathematics	Standard 4	19	6
5	Bahasa Malaysia	Standard 4	10	4
6	English language	Standard 5	9	4
7	Science	Standard 5	9	4
8	Mathematics	Standard 5	10	4
9	Science	Standard 6	9	4
10	Mathematics	Standard 6	10	4
11	Citizenship training	Standard 4-6	19	6
12	World of Education	Teachers	10	2

Schools Radio broadcasts Form 6 programmes in Economics, the General Paper and Hisotry.

7   ADMINISTRATION

The Educational Media Service is a division within the Ministry of Education.

It is headed by a Director who is assisted by a Deputy Director. The EMS is divided into 4 sections.
1)   Educational Television Section;
2)   Educational Radio Section;
3)   Audio-Visual Aids Section;
4)   Administration Section.

The administration section incorporates the publications unit, the evaluation and utilisation unit, and the subject-matter unit.

EMS is structured as shown in figure 4.

TABLE 6.1b   School broadcast output: Secondary school

Series		Level	Language used	No. of pro- grammes	No. of times each pro- gramme will be broadcast
1	Science	Form I	B. Malaysia	19	6
2	Science	Form I	English	19	6
3	Mathema- tics	Form I	B. Malaysia	19	6
4	Mathema- tics	Form I	English	19	7
5	Commercial studies	Form I	B. Malaysia	19	4
6	Science	Form II	B. Malaysia	19	5
7	Science	Form II	English	19	7
8	Mathema- tics	Form II	B. Malaysia	19	7
9	Mathema- tics	Form II	English	19	7
10	Commercial studies	Form II	B. Malaysia	10	4
11	Science	Form III	B. Malaysia	10	7
12	Science	Form III	English	9	7
13	Mathema-	Form III	B. Malaysia	10	5
14	Mathema-	Form III	English	9	5
15	Commercial studies	Form III	B. Malaysia	10	4
16	Civics	Form I-III	B. Malaysia	19	7
17	Science	Form VI	B. Malaysia		4
18	World of Education	Teachers	B. Malaysia	10	4

TABLE 6.2   Breakdown of educational programmes for 1974

Language	Level	No. of programmes
Bahasa	Primary	16
Malaysia	Secondary	14
	General	1
Total		31
English	Primary	13
	Secondary	13
	General	1
Total		27
Chinese	Primary	14
	Secondary	3
	General	1
Total		18
Tamil	Primary	14
	Secondary	3
	General	1
Total		18
General Total:		94

Top management personnel in EMS are ex-teachers, head-masters, etc. They are normally appointed by the Ministry of Education and the criteria is mainly that these teachers should have some kind of media background.

While some of the professional staff are teachers who have received special training, some of the staff are seconded from the Ministry of Information. This especially applies to the professional and technical staff of ETV.

Those officers seconded from the Ministry of Information are paid according to the salary scheme of the Ministry of Information. The salary scheme for EMS officers is not available. It is probably much the same as that of the Ministry of Information as they both belong to the same public service salary scheme.

The staff of EMS who were originally teachers can still

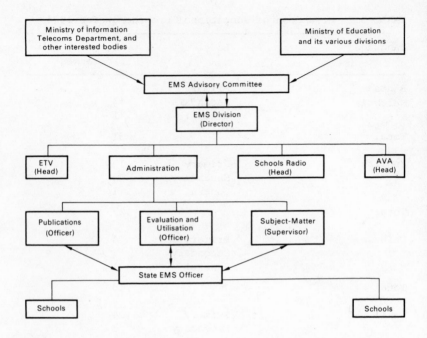

FIGURE 4   Structure of EMS

retain membership of the National Union of Teachers (NUT).
They can also be members of the Congress of Unions of
Employees in Public and Civil Services (CUEPACS). As yet,
employees of EMS do not have a union of their own. There
is no formal relationship to speak of between the administration and the staff of EMS. Representations of complaints, etc. are normally directed to the Ministry of
Education.

8   TRAINING

Training by EMS is limited. Normally, personnel are
chosen who have the necessary experience and ability in
work related to broadcasting. 'On-the-job' training is,
however, provided. There are a number of foreign experts
who provide some of this On-the-job training, while
helping out in the production of programmes.

Before the ETV service was launched, some officers from
the Ministry of Education and Ministry of Information were
sent on a course in educational television production in

the United Kingdom (CETO/CEDO), Australia (ABC) and in
Japan (NHK). With the launching of ETV, a few programmes
to train officers of ETV were arranged.
They are:
(a)   Anglo-Malaysian Education Collaboration Programme
      (AMEC) in the United Kingdom;
(b)   United Nations Development Programme (UNDP);
(c)   National Broadcasting Training Centre (NBTC) at
      Jalan Ampang, Kuala Lumpur.

As from July 1975, the Educational Technology Unit in
the Centre of Educational Studies and the Mass Communication Programme in the School of Humanities, Universiti
Sains Malaysia, has been conducting a one-year certificate
course in educational broadcasting for incoming personnel
of EMS. The course includes the basics of radio and television production to curriculum development. In addition
to this one-year course, there are plans to introduce
short three months' courses for serving officers of EMS.

9   RESEARCH

The Evaluation and Utilisation Unit within the Administration Section of EMS is responsible for research into the
effectiveness of ETV and Schools Radio. The Unit is at
present headed by two officers. The main function of the
unit is to receive feedback from teachers and to send this
to the producers and subject-matter panel concerned to
determine whether the programmes broadcast have achieved
the objectives required by the schools or whether there are
any weaknesses in the programmes that can be corrected.

The unit also prepares evaluation forms for teachers
and students, receives reports from State EMS organisers,
visits schools together with producers and subject advisors to observe the reception of ETV and Schools Radio
programmes and liaises with the publications unit to pre-
pare back-up printed materials for the schools.

The only regular form of research is the compilation
and analysis of evaluation forms from teachers. The data
collected is computerised and fed back to producers and
subject-matter panels and advisors.

There is no immediate plan to launch other types of
research.

Chapter 7

ORGANISATION AND PROCESSES OF REDIFFUSION

Rediffusion is a wired broadcasting station, its parent body being Rediffusion International Limited, London. As a commercial enterprise, it aims to maximise profits for its shareholders by reaching the largest possible audience with programmes that will satisfy as many people as possible.

Rediffusion has stations in Penang, Ipoh and Kuala Lumpur. As it relays programmes by cable, coverage is limited to the areas within the three main towns it operates from.

The Penang station has a coverage of about 8 miles radius and about 11,688 subscribers. The Ipoh station has a coverage of about 6 miles radius with about 7,306 subscribers. The Kuala Lumpur station has a coverage of about 8 miles radius with about 22,868 subscribers.

Rediffusion broadcasts over two networks - Gold and Silver. Each network broadcasts for 18 hours per day. The Gold network broadcasts mainly Chinese programmes whereas the Silver network broadcasts in Bahasa Malaysia, Chinese and English.

The overall breakdown of programme content per week is as follows:

news	15%
information	5%
drama	50%
entertainment	30%

The proportion of foreign as opposed to local programmes is as follows:

	Local	Imported
news	100%	-
information	80%	20%
drama	30%	70%
entertainment	90%	10%

Rediffusion, naturally, is subject to the laws of the country. It has a Board of Directors responsible for its operation and a government representative sits on the Board. At present, this post is filled by the Director-General of Broadcasting.

The government can make use of Rediffusion for its own purposes. It is also formally required that Rediffusion carries news broadcasts from Radio and Television Malaysia for two hours daily. Rediffusion does not, however, have to relay public service announcements or any other programmes from RTM unless specifically requested to do so by the government.

Rediffusion does not produce any programmes on development, religion or programmes with political content. It does, however, co-operate closely with the Department of Broadcasting concerning the relay of government developmental programmes. In most cases Rediffusion will only broadcast RTM programmes or public service announcements if RTM provides the tapes of the programmes or announcements. If it is in the interests of the community, Rediffusion will make public service announcements, particularly for the Public Utilities and Police Departments.

The Divisional Manager of wired broadcasting is responsible for public relations activities of Rediffusion. But Rediffusion does not participate in joint activities with voluntary organisations or specific interest groups other than on a commercial basis. It participates in international broadcasting operations and organisations through its parent company, Rediffusion International Limited in London.

The main sources of income are from subscription fees and advertising revenue. There are also other sources of income such as renting television sets, etc. (Figures of income are not revealed.)

Rediffusion's main areas of expenditure are:
(a) payment for the renting of programmes (from abroad and local);

(b)   operating costs;
(c)   administrative expenses;
(d)   selling expenses.

Rediffusion relays news from RTM. Information/educational programmes account for 5 per cent of the total broadcast. Local programmes from RTM are given greater priority over others from other sources.

Drama, which accounts for 50 per cent of the overall programme content, forms the largest item for broadcast. Most of the drama programmes are imported from Singapore, Hong Kong or Taiwan.

The second largest item, entertainment, accounts for 30 per cent of the overall programme content. Most of these entertainment programmes are locally produced by Rediffusion and supplemented by those imported from Singapore.

Imported English-language programmes are normally purchased from BBC (London) and ABC (Australia) or are obtained from Rediffusion stations in other parts of the world. The imported Chinese-language programmes are from Singapore, Hong Kong and Taiwan. The costs of these programmes are not available.

Technical services are the responsibility of a Chief Engineer, who is directly responsibly to the General Manager. Under the Chief Engineer are the Equipment Supervisors in charge of the various stations. Each Equipment Supervisor will have under his charge a number of technicians.

There are three studios in the Penang station while the Kuala Lumpur station has six studios. The Penang station has a control room for transmission and associated activities. The Kuala Lumpur station has, in addition to the Control Room, a Recording Room whereby all programmes produced in the studios are recorded directly. The Ipoh station has only a Control Room for transmission. It has no production facilities.

The Kuala Lumpur station is also the headquarters of the Malaysian Rediffusion Limited Company, with stations at Penang and Ipoh and offices in Butterworth, Kota Bharu and Alor Star.

The organisational structure is as shown in figure 5.

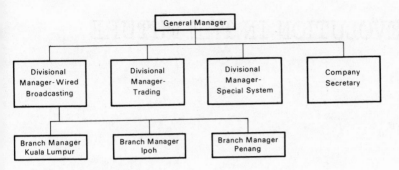

FIGURE 5   Organisational structure of Rediffusion

The head office at Kuala Lumpur administers all the branches through Branch Managers who are consulted concerning all matters relating to their locations. This includes recruitment, finance, training and programming.

The staff is recruited through advertising and by direct application to headquarters in Kuala Lumpur. The professional staff must have broadcasting experience and are normally expected to have passed the Malaysian Certificate Examination. The senior administrative positions are normally filled through the promotion of existing staff, though there is a tendency lately to recruit graduates from local universities. Promotion of senior staff is based on performance. Promotion opportunities for other members of the staff are limited.

The salary scheme is confidential but it has been revealed that the salaries paid are competitive to those paid by government broadcasting agencies.

Employees of Rediffusion are members of the Rediffusion Workers Union of Malaysia. In addition to this, members of the staff also belong to different professional bodies in their individual capacity.

Chapter 8

EVOLUTION IN THE FUTURE

1 NEW PROGRAMMES

Television Malaysia will, in the near future, broadcast a
wide range of new programmes with its primary role being
one of promoting national consciousness and unity, based
on the Rukunegara. The focus will be on public education
in civic consciousness.

Some of the syndicated film series which will be shown
are science fiction series, such as 'Planet of the Apes',
or films based on well-known novels such as the 'Great
Mysteries' series and 'Born Free'. In addition, children's programmes and other educational series such as
'Wild, Wild World of Animals', and 'World of Medicine'
will be shown. Cultural programmes and documentaries are
also expected to come from the ASEAN (Indonesia, Singapore, Thailand, and the Philippines) countries and also
Egypt.

Television Malaysia also hopes to undertake more regional reporting through the use of their Outside Broadcasting (OB) mobile units from 1975. These programmes will
not only be tapping local cultural festivals or entertainment, but will also include documentaries on the progress
of other Malaysian states in their factories, community
development, cottage industries, etc. By so doing, Television Malaysia will have more programmes for rural
viewers. In planning their future programmes, Television
Malaysia Network II recently started their broadcasts
earlier at 6 p.m., because the rural viewers start their
working day at 5 or 6 a.m. and go to bed at about 10 p.m.

2   GOING COLOUR

Television Malaysia will be forced to introduce colour
transmission because the world trend is towards colour
television. It is no longer feasible for Malaysia to continue with black and white (monochrome) television as this
equipment will have to be specially ordered which would be
very expensive.

Television Malaysia has a three-phase plan to bring
colour television to the country which will take about
seven years. It is hoped that complete colour transmission will be possible by 1982-3.

The first phase, - with limited colour transmissions of
syndicated films - is expected to begin by the end of 1975
or at the latest in 1976. It will include converting or
replacing the monochrome equipment. Certain monochrome
equipment is 'colour compatible' and only certain parts
need to be changed to be able to handle colour transmissions. Since 1969, Television Malaysia has been forced
by circumstances to use colour compatible transmitters.
The non-colour transmitters being used at present are due
for replacement. So the switch to colour comes at an
appropriate time. During this phase, technical staff will
be trained to handle colour transmissions.

The second phase includes the conversion of Television
Malaysia studios to make them suitable for colour transmissions. At this stage limited local colour productions
will be introduced.

The third phase which will end sometime in 1982 or
1983, will effect complete colour transmission. The
colour transmission will not affect monochrome television
sets. This is because of the compatible nature of the
colour transmission adopted. All colour information is
transmitted within the same bandwidth as the monochrome
information.

3   NATIONAL TRANSMISSION VIA SATELLITE

Television Malaysia was scheduled (at the time of
writing) to have its first transmission by the end of
August 1975, which would cover all the states in Peninsular Malaysia as well as Sabah and Sarawak in East Malaysia. The simultaneous broadcasts will go through the
earth satellite station in Kuantan and be relayed via

the Intelsat III satellite over the Indian Ocean to the
earth station in Kota Kinabalu, Sabah.

Initially, only one network will go national and broadcasts will begin at about 8.30 p.m. daily (Peninsular
Time) but the number of hours had not yet been decided at
the time of writing. Because of the half-hour difference
between the Peninsular Standard Time and the East Malaysia
Time, a lot of programme planning has to be done.

Malaysia, as a new member of the satellite community,
is lacking in many aspects of satellite technology and
also faces the additional problem of high costs. It is
hoped that the governing body of the International Communications Satellite Consortium, Intelsat, will devise a
new formula whereby the rates of hiring satellites are
within the financial abilities of the poor and developing
nations.

Communication officials in Malaysia feel that the use
of satellites should not be calculated on a commercial
scale, but should be considered as a programme for the
promotion of peace throughout the world. Constant and
regular exchanges of live television programmes between
countries would be a way of promoting world peace. This
is increasingly important in Malaysia's efforts to combat
the present trend of television production houses concen-
trating on entertainment.

Chapter 9

COMMUNICATION POLICIES

Even though there is no official national communication
policy, Malaysia does have certain clear guidelines for
planning and implementing its communication activities.
However, some communicators in Malaysia feel that a
greater co-ordination between the various government and
non-government agencies involved in communication is
desirable. It is also the opinion of many that a coherent
and long-range national policy in the field of communication would be beneficial to the growth of communication
facilities and would more effectively support the social,
economic and cultural development programmes.

Communication policies exist in Malaysia on an ad-hoc
basis. In addition, most of the policies are not officially written or formulated, since policies should
ideally be flexible and also they change with time.
Integration and co-ordination of communication activities
in Malaysia are also done on an ad-hoc and short-term
basis depending on the need and the project (e.g. road
safety campaigns, applied nutrition campaigns, etc.).
A national, on-going, and comprehensive communication
policy so as to determine the rights, interests, obliga-
tions, and interdependence of various communication
institutions or agencies with communication components
within society is still to be formulated.

The existence of several Laws and Acts and the fact
that almost all of the mass media outlets (except for
Rediffusion, RAAF and some newspapers and magazines) are
government-owned, could also be considered as some of
the implicit national communication policies to reduce or
avoid internal contradictions as well as to safeguard the
rights and interests of various sectors of the society.

Some of the policy makers in the field of communication in Malaysia are now trying to formulate a national communication policy which will provide the framework for anticipating changes in media technology, assessing their value for promoting national and international goals, and revealing any possible harmful effects.

Policies which attempt to regulate the excessive inflow of foreign content programmes have been formulated but only in very general terms.   However, there is no 'filtering' policy yet, even though there are general criteria as to what content programmes show.

At presemt, most of the communication policies' formulation and the planning for communication activities is done at the highest level of the Ministry of Information and at Cabinet level. Communication strategy and management planning is done within the Ministry of Information. Implementation is done by the various sections of the two departments of the Ministry of Information, the Department of Broadcasting and the Department of Information Services. It is at this level that more integration and co-ordination would be beneficial.

A national communication policy should be formulated in order to avoid duplication of activities and to delegate tasks and responsibilities. At a communication workshop held in June 1975 by the Ministry of Information in collaboration with the Communication Programme of the University of Science Malaysia, it was recommended that a Communication Data Bank (or a Communication Planning Unit) be established. This could be useful in determining a comprehensive and sound communication plan and strategy with the necessary co-ordination and integration with other government and/or non-government agencies.

However, it is still to be seen whether systematic communication planning at the national level, upon which communication policies can be formulated to enable implementation, is too complicated and politically impracticable. Some people believe that systems approaches to planning might be thought helpful at the programme or project level within an area of communication, such as expanding radio broadcasting, but the inputs, variables, and especially the external, environmental uncertainties become so complex at more general levels that a systems approach may be thought useless. This would imply that national level communication policies and planning, if not left to chance and the product of competing pressures and interests, was at least an art, if not a science, to be approached systematically and theoretically.

APPENDIX

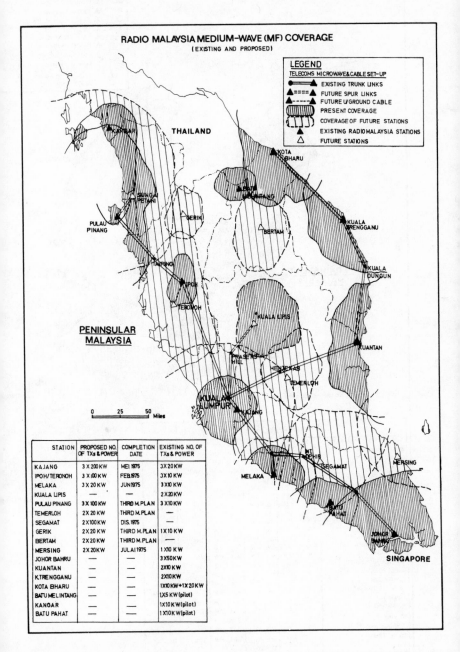

RADIO MALAYSIA MEDIUM-WAVE (MF) COVERAGE
(EXISTING AND PROPOSED)

LEGEND

TELECOMS MICROWAVE & CABLE SET-UP

- EXISTING TRUNK LINKS
- FUTURE SPUR LINKS
- FUTURE U/GROUND CABLE
- PRESENT COVERAGE
- COVERAGE OF FUTURE STATIONS
- ▲ EXISTING RADIO MALAYSIA STATIONS
- △ FUTURE STATIONS

THAILAND

PENINSULAR MALAYSIA

SINGAPORE

STATION	PROPOSED NO. OF TXs & POWER	COMPLETION DATE	EXISTING NO. OF TXs & POWER
KAJANG	3 X 200 KW	MEI 1975	3 X 20 KW
IPOH/TERONOH	3 X 100 KW	FEB.1975	3 X 10 KW
MELAKA	3 X 20 KW	JUN 1975	3 X 10 KW
KUALA LIPIS	—	—	2 X 20 KW
PULAU PINANG	3 X 100 KW	THIRD M. PLAN	3 X 10 KW
TEMERLOH	2 X 20 KW	THIRD M.PLAN	—
SEGAMAT	2 X 100 KW	DIS. 1975	—
GERIK	2 X 20 KW	THIRD M.PLAN	1 X 10 KW
BERTAM	2 X 20 KW	THIRD M.PLAN	—
MERSING	2 X 20 KW	JULAI 1975	1 X 10 KW
JOHOR BAHRU	—	—	3 X 50 KW
KUANTAN	—	—	2 X 10 KW
K.TRENGGANU	—	—	2 X 10 KW
KOTA BHARU	—	—	1 X 10 KW+1 X 20 KW
BATU MELINTANG	—	—	1 X 5 KW (pilot)
KANGAR	—	—	1 X 10 KW(pilot)
BATU PAHAT	—	—	1 X 10 KW(pilot)

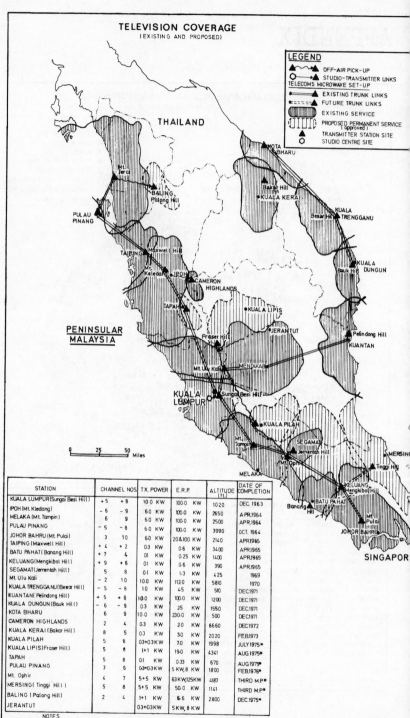

TELEVISION COVERAGE
(EXISTING AND PROPOSED)

LEGEND

Symbol	Description
	OFF-AIR PICK-UP
	STUDIO-TRANSMITTER LINKS
	TELECOMS MICROWAVE SET-UP
	EXISTING TRUNK LINKS
	FUTURE TRUNK LINKS
	EXISTING SERVICE
	PROPOSED PERMANENT SERVICE (approved)
	TRANSMITTER STATION SITE
	STUDIO CENTRE SITE

THAILAND

PENINSULAR MALAYSIA

0   25   50 Miles

STATION	CHANNEL NOS		T.X. POWER	E.R.P.	ALTITUDE (ft)	DATE OF COMPLETION
KUALA LUMPUR(Sungai Besi Hill)	+ 5	+ 8	10·0 KW	100·0 KW	1020	DEC. 1963
IPOH (Mt. Kledang)	6	9	6·0 KW	100·0 KW	2650	APR.1964
MELAKA (Mt. Tampin)	6	9	6·0 KW	100·0 KW	2500	APR.1964
PULAU PINANG	5	8	6·0 KW	100·0 KW	3990	OCT. 1964
JOHOR BAHRU (Mt. Pulai)	3	10	6·0 KW	20&100 KW	2140	APR.1965
TAIPING (Maxwell Hill)	+ 4	+ 2	0·3 KW	0·6 KW	3400	APR.1965
BATU PAHAT(Banang Hill)	+ 7	4	0·1 KW	0·25 KW	1400	APR.1965
KELUANG(Mengkibol Hill)	+ 9	+ 6	0·1 KW	0·6 KW	390	APR.1965
SEGAMAT(Jerantah Hill)	5	8	0·1 KW	1·3 KW	425	1969
Mt. Ulu Kali	2	10	10·0 KW	112·0 KW	5810	1970
KUALA TRENGGANU (Besar Hill)	5	8	1·0 KW	45 KW	510	DEC.1971
KUANTAN (Pelindong Hill)	+ 5	+ 8	10·0 KW	100·0 KW	510	DEC.1971
KUALA DUNGUN (Bauk Hill)	6	9	0·3 KW	25 KW	1550	DEC.1971
KOTA BHARU	6	9	10·0 KW	230·0 KW	500	DEC.1971
CAMERON HIGHLANDS	2	4	0·3 KW	2·0 KW	6660	DEC.1972
KUALA KERAI (Bakar Hill)	8	5	0·3 KW	3·0 KW	2020	FEB.1973
KUALA PILAH	5	8	03+03KW	7·0 KW	1998	JULY.1975*
KUALA LIPIS(Fraser Hill)	5	8	1+1 KW	19·0 KW	4341	AUG.1975*
TAPAH	5	8	0·1 KW	0·33 KW	670	AUG.1979*
PULAU PINANG	3	6	03+03KW	5 KW,8 KW		FEB.1976*
Mt. Ophir	4	7	5+5 KW	63KW,125KW	4187	THIRD M.P*
MERSING(Tinggi Hill)	5	8	5+5 KW	50·0 KW	1141	THIRD M.P*
BALING (Palong Hill)	2	4	1+1 KW	6·6 KW	2800	DEC.1975*
JERANTUT			03+03KW	5KW, 8 KW		

NOTES

1 CHANNEL ALLOCATIONS AND SITES FOR FUTURE STATIONS ARE TENTATIVE
2 '+' AND '-' PREFIXED TO CHANNEL NUMBERS INDICATES 10KHz CARRIER OFF-SET WORKING
3 E.R.P = EFFECTIVE RADIATED POWER
4 * = PROPOSED SERVICE

BIBLIOGRAPHY

DYER, FRANCES, 'The Print and Broadcasting Media in
Malaysia', South East Asia Press Centre, Kuala Lumpur,
1974.

GLATTBACH, JACK and ANDERSON, MIKE, 'The Print and Broadcasting Media in Malaysia', South East Asia Press Centre,
Kuala Lumpur, 1971.

GOVERNMENT OF MALAYSIA, 'Second Malaysia Plan 1971-1975',
Government Printers, Kuala Lumpur, 1971.

GOVERNMENT OF MALAYSIA, 'Highlights of the Second Malaysia
Plan', statement by the Prime Minister at a press conference at the National Operations Room, Kuala Lumpur,
27 May 1971. Government Printers, Kuala Lumpur, 1973.

GOVERNMENT OF MALAYSIA, 'Monthly Statistical Bulletin of
West Malaysia', Government Printers, Kuala Lumpur, 1974.

GOVERNMENT OF MALAYSIA, 'Malaysia Official Book, 1974',
Government Printers, Kuala Lumpur.

HANCOCK, ALAN, 'The Development of Educational Mass Media
in Malaysia', 1971 (Revised). Ministry of Education:
Educational Media Service, a report, Publications Unit,
EMS, 1975.

LIM, PETER, 'Basic Readings in Malaysian Economics',
Modern Educational Publishers, Kuala Lumpur, 1972.

MALAYSIA, THE TREASURY, Economic Report 1974 - 1975,
Government Printers, Kuala Lumpur, 1974.

MOHAMMAD GHAZALI SHAFIE, 'Rakyat Malaysia Baru', speech
by the Minister of Special Affairs and Information, Tan
Sri Mohammad Ghazali Shafie at the Dewan Negara, Kuala
Lumpur, 2 August 1971. Published by Government Printers.

NEW STRAITS TIMES PRESS, Malaysia Year Book, 1974, Kuala
Lumpur.

ROGERS, MARVIN, Malaysia/Singapore: Problem and Challenges of the 70's in 'Asia Survey', vol. II, no. 2,
Feb. 1971.

RTM 1973 HANDOUTS

RYAN, N.J., 'The Making of Modern Malaysia and Singapore', Oxford University Press, Kuala Lumpur, 1969.

37·302